KNOWING YOUR ENEMY

Be Sober, Be Alert

BRIAN HICKS

Knowing Your Enemy
by Ps. Brian Hicks

Published by:
World Harvest Ministries,
PO Box 90, Bald Hills, Qld, 4036, Australia
whm.org.au

This book or parts thereof may not be reproduced in any form, stored in a retrieval system, or transmitted in any form, by any means - electronic, mechanical, photocopy, recording or otherwise - without prior written permission of the author or publisher, except as provided by Australian copyright law.

All scriptural references are taken from the Application Bible or the Ryrie Study Bible unless otherwise stated.

Cover Design by Sarah Freeman

Copyright © Brian Hicks

First Published October 2020

ISBN: 978-0-6485897-4-7

THIS BOOK IS DEDICATED TO
ENLIGHTENING BELIEVERS BY EXPOSING THE
WORKS OF DARKNESS

This subject is not to bring fear, but rather to make us aware of Satan's schemes and to recognise that he is not the all-powerful one, but a created one. God has given us (the Church) the power to overcome in Jesus Christ.

FOREWORD

Many years ago, while I was on television, my program "The Winners Way," was airing in local prisons and correctional centres. Inmates began to write to me, and one particular prisoner requested a visit. Because of Pastor Brian's unique life journey, I asked Pastor Brian if he would visit this prisoner on my behalf. From this visit was birthed our Prison Chaplaincy Ministry.

Brian has now been visiting the correctional centres of South East Queensland for the last 20 years. During this time, Pastor Brian has witnessed firsthand the destructive power of the enemy on people's lives and their families. He has also witnessed the life changing power of the gospel of the Lord Jesus Christ firsthand. Hundreds of men have been encouraged, comforted and found Christ. This work still continues to this day.

Brian has an amazing testimony, and I have helped him produce this book, from his bible college study notes and firsthand experience of the work of the kingdom of darkness. In this book, you will learn about the existence of Satan and his nature. Through many biblical references from the word of God, you will be able to learn where demons come from and how you can have authority over Satan and the evil forces of darkness.

I highly recommend this work to every scholar of the bible, who desires to understand how the kingdom of darkness works and how to take authority over these evil, destructive forces.

I am reminded of that quotes by Sun Tzu, "Know the enemy and know yourself; in a hundred battles, you will never be in peril. When you are ignorant of the enemy, but know yourself, your chances of winning or losing are equal. If ignorant both of your enemy and yourself, you are certain in every battle to be in peril."-Sun Tzu, The Art of War

God Bless,

Dr. Shaun Marler
Author of 'Life Changing Principles for Victorious Living',
Senior Pastor of World Harvest Ministries, Brisbane, Australia.

Acknowledgements

Scripture References are taken from:

King James Bible

The Application Bible

The Ryrie Study Bible – New American Standard

Study Notes are taken from:

The Application Bible

References appearing within this manual written as such: Eg. 'Text page 167' refer to material sourced from the book, **"*Angelology*" by C. Fred Dickason.**

THANK YOU

Pastor Brian Hicks would like to extend his appreciation to the following people who assisted with the typing and final production of this book:

Kelly Taylor

Robyn Hall

Sarah Freeman

Contents

Introduction	15
Chapter One THE ORIGIN OF SATAN	33
Chapter Two THE FALL OF LUCIFER	51
Chapter Three THE PERSONALITY OF SATAN	63
Chapter Four SPECIFIC NAMES APPLIED TO SATAN	69
Chapter Five THE ORIGIN OF DEMONS	99
Chapter Six SATAN'S PRESENT POWER AND ACTIVITY	103
Chapter Seven THE REALITY OF DEMONS	115
Chapter Eight THE DERIVATION OF DEMONS	121
Chapter Nine THE DESCRIPTION OF DEMONS	127
Chapter Ten THE DUTIES OF DEMONS	131
Chapter Eleven DOMINATION OF DEMONS	141
Chapter Twelve THE OCCULT	157
Chapter Thirteen THE DEFEAT AND DESTINY OF SATAN AND HIS DEMONS	167
Chapter Fourteen THE DEFENCE OF BELIEVERS AGAINST SATAN AND DEMONS	173
CONCLUSION	177

Knowing Your Enemy

Introduction

୫୨ ଓଷ

Why are we undertaking Bible Studies?

Firstly we want to be a good servant in Christ.

2 Timothy 4:6-16 says,

> v. 6, 'For I am now ready to be offered and the time of my departure is at hand.
>
> v. 7, I have fought a good fight, I have finished my course, I have kept the faith:
>
> v. 8, In the future there is laid up for me a crown of righteousness, which the Lord the righteous judge shall give me at that day: and not to me only but also to all who have loved his appearing.

v. 9, *Make every effort to come to me soon;*

v. 10, *For Demas has deserted me, having loved this present world and has departed to Thessalonica; Crescens to Galatia, Titus to Dalmatia.*

v. 11, *Only Luke is with me. Take Mark and bring him with you: for he is profitable to me for the ministry.*

v. 12, *And Tychicus I have sent to Ephesus.*

v. 13, *The cloak that I left at Troas with Carpus, when you come, bring with you the books, but especially the parchments.*

v. 14, *Alexander the coppersmith did me much harm: the Lord reward (repay) him according to his works (deeds):*

v. 15, *Be on guard against him yourself; for he has greatly opposed our words.*

v. 16, *At my first defence no man stood with me, but all men deserted me: I pray God that it may not be counted against them.'*

Secondly, to be teachers and examples.

1. We need to be taught, so we may teach others.
In 2 Timothy 2:2 Paul says, 'And the things that you have heard of me among many witnesses, the same you commit to faithful men, who shall be able to teach others also.'

2. Paul is encouraging believers who are taught in the word, that they, in turn, are to reproduce themselves. Disciples need to be equipped so that they can pass on their faith, and their work is not done until new believers are able to make disciples of others.

3. Look at Ephesians 4:12, 13,

> *v. 12,* **'For the perfecting of the saints,** *for the work of the ministry, for the edifying of the body of Christ:*

> *v. 13, Till we all come in the unity of the faith and of the knowledge of the Son of God, to a perfect man, to the measure of the stature of the fullness of Christ.'*

I believe that what we learn through this study, we will be able to teach others, so they, as the scripture says, will no longer be infants, tossed back and forth by the waves.

God has given us an enormous responsibility to make disciples in every nation starting from here. Look at Matthew 28:18-20, *v. 18, 'And Jesus came and spoke to them saying, All power is given to Me in heaven and in earth.*

v. 19, Go therefore and teach all nations, baptizing them in the name of the Father, and of the Son and of the Holy Ghost:

v. 20, Teaching them to observe all things whatsoever I have commanded you; and remember, I am with you always, even unto the end of the world. Amen.'

This involves:
1. Preaching
2. Teaching
3. Healing
4. Nurturing
5. Giving
6. Administering
7. Building and many other tasks

If we had to fulfill this command as individuals, we might as well give up without trying; it would be impossible. God calls us as members of His body. Some of us are able to do one task; some are able to do another. Together we can obey God more fully than any of us could do alone.

Look at Ephesians 4:4,

v. 4, 'There is one body and one Spirit, even as you are called in one hope of your calling.'

Read Genesis 3:1-24,

v. 1, 'Now the serpent was more subtle than any beast of the field which the Lord God had made. And he said to the woman, Yea, has God said you shall not eat of every tree of the garden?

v. 2, And the woman said to the serpent, we may eat of the fruit of the trees of the garden;

v. 3, But of the fruit of the tree which is in the midst of the garden, God has said, You shall not eat of it, neither shall you touch it, lest you die.

v. 4, And the serpent said to the woman, You shall not surely die:

v. 5, For God knows that in the day you eat of it, then your eyes shall be opened and you shall be as gods, knowing good and evil.

v. 6, And when the woman saw that the tree was good for food and that it was pleasant to the eyes and a tree to be desired to make one wise, she took of the fruit and ate and gave also to her husband with her; and he ate.

v. 7, And the eyes of them both were opened and they knew that they were naked and they sewed fig leaves together, and made themselves aprons.

v. 8, And they heard the voice of the Lord God walking in the garden in the cool of the day: and Adam and his wife hid themselves from the presence of the Lord God amongst the trees of the garden.

v. 9, And the Lord God called to Adam and said to him, Where are you?

v. 10, And he said, I heard Your voice in the garden and I was afraid because I was naked; and I hid myself.

v. 11, And He said, Who told you that you were naked? Have you eaten of the tree, which I commanded that you should not eat?

v. 12, And the man said, The woman who You gave to be with me, she gave me of the tree, and I ate.

v. 13, And the Lord God said to the woman, What is this that you have done? And the woman said, The serpent beguiled me and I ate.

v. 14, And the Lord God said unto the serpent, Because you have done this, you are cursed above all cattle and above every beast of the field; upon your belly you shall go and dust you will eat all the days of your life:

v. 15, And I will put enmity between you and the woman and between your seed and her seed; it shall bruise your head, and you shall bruise his heel.

v. 16, Unto the woman He said, I will greatly multiply your sorrow and your conception; in sorrow you shall bring forth children; and your desire shall be for your husband and he shall rule over you.

v. 17, And to Adam He said, Because you have listened to the voice of your wife and have eaten of the tree which I commanded you, saying you shall not eat of it: cursed is the ground because of you; in sorrow (toil) you shall eat of it all the days of your life;

v. 18, Thorns also and thistles it will bring forth for you and you shall eat the herb of the field;

v. 19, In the sweat of your face shall you eat bread, till you return to the ground; for out of it you were taken: for you are dust and to dust you shall return.

v. 20, And Adam called his wife's name Eve, because she was the mother of all living.

v. 21, *Unto Adam also and to his wife the Lord God made coats of skins and clothed them.*

v. 22, *And the Lord God said, Behold, the man is become as one of us, to know good and evil: and now, lest he put forth his hand and take also of the tree of life, and eat and live for ever:*

v. 23, *Therefore the Lord God sent him forth from the Garden of Eden, to till the ground from which he was taken.*

v. 24, *So he drove out the man and he placed at the east of the garden of Eden Cherubims, and a flaming sword which turned every way, to guard the way to the tree of life.'*

Why do we need to know the existence of Satan?

Let's read 1 Peter 5:8,

'Be sober, be vigilant; because your adversary the devil, as a roaring lion walks about, seeking whom he may devour.'

The answer to this question is, that as we can see, Satan roams around like a roaring lion seeking to devour the unsuspecting, so we need to be aware of his schemes. The Bible warns us of this.

If we look at 2 Cor. 2:11,

> *'Lest Satan should get an advantage of us: for we are not ignorant of his devices.'*

So now, we will go and look at what the Bible teaches us about Satan.

Genesis 3:1 says,

> *'Now the serpent was more subtle (crafty) than any beast of the field which the Lord God had made. And he said unto the woman, Has God said you shall not eat of every tree of the garden?'*

Satan, at one time, was a created angel who rebelled against God and was thrown out of Heaven. We will see this through the scriptures as we continue with our studies.

We find Satan, as a created being, has definite limitations. Because he is created not divine, he is not omnipresent, he can not be everywhere, whereas God is. He is not omnipotent, all-powerful and he is not all-knowing.

One of Satan's main goals is to keep mankind from knowing God. We can see that Satan came to Eve disguised as a crafty serpent; that is why he was also called the angel of light, he comes like God with his temptations.

Although he is trying to tempt everyone away from God, he will not be the final victor. In Genesis 4:14-15, God promises that Satan will be crushed by one of the woman's offspring, which is talking of the Messiah (Jesus).

So from the beginning of humanity, Satan has been the tempter.

Why does Satan tempt us?

The answer is: Temptation is Satan's invitation to give into his kind of life and give up on God's kind of life.

Satan tempted Eve and succeeded in getting her to sin. Ever since then, he's been busy getting people to sin.

Now, we sin because we are sinners, we don't sin and become sinners. We are sinners because of Eve's sin.

That's why Jesus said we must be born again. Read John 3:1-8,

> v. 1, 'There was a man of the Pharisees, named Nicodemus, a ruler of the Jews:
>
> v. 2, The same came to Jesus by night and said to Him, Rabbi, we know that You are a teacher come from God: for no man can do these miracles that you do, except God be with him.
>
> v. 3, Jesus answered and said to him, Verily, verily I say to you, except a man be born again, he cannot see the kingdom of God.

v. 4, Nicodemus said to Him, How can a man be born when he is old? Can he enter a second time into his mother's womb and be born?

v. 5, Jesus answered, Verily, verily, I say to you, except a man be born of water and of the spirit, he cannot enter into the kingdom of God.

v. 6, That which is born of the flesh is flesh and that which is born of the Spirit is spirit.

v. 7, Do not marvel that I said to you, you must be born again.'

v. 8, The wind blows where it wishes and you hear the sound of it, but cannot tell where it comes from, and where is goes; so is every one that is born of the Spirit.

When we become born again, we have to learn how to walk again with God, by our new nature.

Look at Romans 8:14, 'For as many as are led by the Spirit of God, they are the sons of God.'

Also in Galatians 5:16-23, it says,

v. 16, 'This I say then, walk in the spirit and you shall not fulfil the lusts of the flesh.

v. 17, For the flesh lusts against the Spirit and Spirit against the flesh and these are contrary the one to the other: so that you cannot do the things that you would.

v. 18, But if you are led of the Spirit, you are not under the law.

v. 19, Now the works of the flesh are manifest, which are these, Adultery, fornication, uncleanness, lasciviousness,

v. 20, Idolatry, witchcraft, hatred, variance, emulations, wrath, strife, seditions, heresies,

v. 21, Envyings, murders, drunkenness, revellings and such like: of which I told you before, as I have also told you in time past, that they who do such things shall not inherit the kingdom of God.

v. 22, But the fruit of the Spirit is love, joy, peace, patience, kindness, goodness, faith.

v. 23, Gentleness, self control; against such there is no law.'

How could Eve have resisted temptation?

The Answer is, by following the same guidelines we can follow.

Firstly we must realize that being tempted is not sin. It's when we yield to the temptation that it becomes a sin.

To resist sin, temptation, we must:

a) Pray for strength to resist. If Eve had done this, it might have been a very different story.

b) Run from sin, sometimes literally. Look at Proverbs 22:3, *'A prudent man foresees the evil and hides himself: but the simple pass on and are punished.'* (KJV)

c) Say no, when confronted with what we know is wrong. James 1:12 tells us of the blessings and rewards for those who don't give in when tempted.

> *v. 12, 'Blessed is the man that endures temptation: for when he is tried, he shall receive the crown of life, which the Lord has promised to them that love Him.'*

Satan attacks us through our weaknesses.

a) Satan tempted Eve by getting her to doubt God's goodness.

b) Satan implied that God was strict, stingy and selfish for not wanting Eve to share his knowledge of GOOD and EVIL.

c) Satan made Eve forget all that God had given her and instead, had her focus on the one thing she could not have.

This is the same trick he tries on us, when we dwell on the few things we don't have rather than on the countless things God has given us.

Let us look at Hebrews 13:5-6,

> *v. 5, 'Let your conversation be without covetousness; and be content with such things as you have: for He has said, I will never leave you, nor forsake you.*
>
> *v. 6, So that we may boldly say, The Lord is my helper and I will not fear what man shall do to me.'*

Satan constantly tries to replace right with wrong.

Satan tried to make Eve think that sin is good, pleasant and desirable. And that knowledge of both good and evil, would be harmless to her.

People usually choose the wrong things because they become convinced that those things are good, at least for themselves. Our sins do not always appear ugly to us, and the pleasant sins are the hardest to avoid.

Let's look again at Galatians 5:16 – 21,

> *v. 16, 'This I say then, walk in the spirit and you shall not fulfil the lusts of the flesh.*

v. 17, For the flesh lusts against the Spirit and Spirit against the flesh and these are contrary the one to the other: so that you cannot do the things that you would.

v. 18, But if you be led of the Spirit, you are not under the law.

v. 19, Now the works of the flesh are manifest, which are these, Adultery, fornication, uncleanness, lasciviousness,

v. 20, Idolatry, witchcraft, hatred, variance, emulations, wrath, strife, seditions, heresies,

v. 21, Envyings, murders, drunkenness, revellings and such like: of which I told you before, as I have also told you in time past, they which do such things shall not inherit the kingdom of God.'

These scriptures show us that we are able to prepare ourselves to resist the attractive temptations that may come our way.

We cannot always prevent temptation, but there is always an escape.

1 Corinthians 10:13 says, 'There has no temptation taken you but such as is common to man:

> but God is faithful, who will not allow you to be tempted above what you are able; but will, with the temptation also make a way to escape, that you may be able to bear it.'

Satan is our enemy; he will do anything he can to get us to follow his evil, deadly path.

In Genesis 3:14 and 15, God was revealing His plan to defeat Satan and offer salvation to the world through his son Jesus Christ.

> v. 14, 'And the Lord God said to the serpent, Because you have done this, you are cursed above all cattle and above every beast of the field; upon your belly you shall go and dust shall you eat all the days of your life;

> v. 15, And I will put enmity between you and the woman and between your seed and her seed; it shall crush your head and you shalt bruise (strike) his heel.'

As we can see, this is referring to Jesus. The phrase, 'You will strike his heel' refers to Satan's repeated attempts to defeat Christ during his life on earth. Whereas the phrase, 'He will crush your head' refers to Satan's defeat when Christ rose from the dead.

A strike on the heel is not deadly, but a crushing blow to the head is.

We need to be aware of Satan's devices. Paul shows us in 2 Corinthians 2:11, where he says these words, 'in order that Satan might not outwit us (take advantage of us), **for we are not ignorant of his schemes.**'

KNOWING YOUR ENEMY

Chapter One

The Origin of Satan

In Ezekiel 28:1-19 and Isaiah 14:4-23, we find that the scriptures give a double reference to the person being addressed.

a) In Isaiah, it starts with the King of Babylon and then refers to Lucifer.

b) In Ezekiel, it starts with the Prince and King of Tyre and then refers to Lucifer.

God initially addresses both of these natural rulers, which are a type of Satan and then we find He goes on to address Satan himself.

Firstly we will look at some points concerning the King of Babylon.

1. We find that Babylon is a picture of all that opposes God. Babylon is a type of the world, that is, the world system.

It shows us in the Bible that in the end times, everything that opposes God will be destroyed and evil will be removed from the earth forever.

2. We see in the time of Babylon, that God permitted Babylon to have temporary power for a purpose. The reason was to punish His wayward people. However, when the purpose ended, so did the power.

We must remember that these people knew their wrongs, because when the pressure was applied, they knew where to turn.

It's like us today, we know when we are in rebellion, and God may have to allow something drastic to happen to bring us back to Himself.

Now let us look at Ezekiel 28:1-19,

> v. 1, 'The word of the Lord came again unto me, saying,

> v. 2, Son of man, say unto the prince of Tyrus, thus says the Lord God; Because your heart is lifted up and you have said, I am a God, I sit in the seat of God, in the midst of the seas; yet you are a man and not God, though you set your heart as the heart of God:

v. 3, Behold, you are wiser than Daniel; there is no secret that they can hide from you:

v. 4, With your wisdom and with your understanding, you have gotten riches and have gotten gold and silver into your treasures:

v. 5, By your great wisdom and by your traffic have you increased your riches, and your heart is lifted up because of your riches:

v. 6, Therefore thus says the Lord God, Because you have set your heart as the heart of God;

v. 7, Behold, therefore I will bring strangers upon you, the terrible of the nations: and they shall draw their swords against the beauty of your wisdom and they shall defile your brightness.

v. 8, They shall bring you down to the pit and you shall die the deaths of them that are slain in the midst of the seas.

v. 9, Will you yet say before him that slays you, I am God? But you shall be a man and no God, in the hand of him that slays you.

v. 10, You shall die the deaths of the uncircumcised by the hand of strangers: for I have spoken it, says the Lord God.

v. 11, Moreover the word of the Lord came unto me saying,

v. 12, 'Son of man take up a lamentation upon the king of Tyrus and say unto him, Thus says the Lord God; You seal up the sum, full of wisdom and perfect in beauty.

v. 13, You have been in Eden the garden of God; every precious stone was your covering, the sardius, topaz and the diamond, the beryl, the onyx and the jasper, the sapphire, the emerald and the carbuncle and gold: the workmanship of your tabrets and of thy pipes was prepared in thee in the day that you were created.

v. 14, You are the anointed cherub that covers; and I have set you so: you were upon the holy mountain of God; you hast walked up and down in the midst of the stones of fire.

v. 15, You were perfect in your ways from the day that you were created, till iniquity was found in you.

v. 16, By the multitude of your merchandise they have filled the midst of you with violence and you have sinned: therefore I will cast you as profane out of the mountain of God: and I will destroy you, O covering cherub, from the midst of the stones of fire.

v. 17, Your heart was lifted up because of your beauty, you have corrupted your wisdom by reason of your brightness: I will cast you to the ground, I will lay you before kings, that they may behold you.

v. 18, You have defiled your sanctuaries by the multitude of your iniquities, by the iniquity of your traffic; therefore will I bring forth a fire from the midst of you, it shall devour you and I will bring you to ashes upon the earth in the sight of all them that behold you.

v. 19, All they that know you among the people shall be astonished at you: you shall be a terror and never shall you be any more.

In Ray Allen's manual on Angelology and Demonology, he mentions that history tells us, that "The Prince of Tyre" was Ithoblus II. There is no record in history of there ever being a King of Tyre at that time, so it must have been speaking of some leader over the city.

In the verses above, we can see that judgment is on Tyre and its leader.

But the question is: Do verses 11 to 19 go beyond the human leader to reveal things about something or someone else?

Let's look at some facts leading to these scriptures.

Firstly, we notice in verse 2 that the King of Tyre stepped out of his league. He saw himself as a god.

> v. 2, 'Son of man, say unto the prince of Tyrus, Thus says the Lord God; Because your heart is lifted up and you have said, I am a God, I sit in the seat of God, in the midst of the seas; yet you are a man and not God, though you set your heart as the heart of God...'

We can see God telling him he is not a god but a mere man. This is the same as Satan, he thinks himself as a god but he is not and never will be.

It can be seen in the scriptures that the land of Tyre and the Prince of Tyre are used to give us an inside view of Satan.

Let's have another look at Ezekiel 28:12-19,

The first thing we can see in these scriptures is that Lucifer (Satan) was definitely not created evil; he was created perfect. Look at v. 15,

> v. 15, 'You were perfect in your ways from the day that you were created, till iniquity was found in you.'

We find that the thing responsible for Lucifer's fall was pride.

He was so impressed with himself that he forgot he was a created being; that all his beauty and power came from God. He decided that he was, in fact, better than God and could do a better job of running the universe.

Look what it says in Proverbs 16:18 concerning pride.

> v. 18, 'Pride goes before destruction and a haughty spirit before a fall.'

Tyre was known as the "merchant of the peoples of many coastlands." We find that it increased in wealth and they boasted in it.

> Look at Ezekiel 28:5, 'By your great wisdom and by your traffic have you increased your riches, and your heart is lifted up because of your riches...'

Satan always tries to focus our lives upon our increased wealth. Even the Psalmist recognized the traps that may come from the Devil.

Look at Psalm 62:9-10,

> v. 9, 'Surely men of low degree are vanity and men of high degree are a lie: to be laid in the balance, they are altogether lighter than vanity.
>
> v. 10, 'Trust not in oppression and become not vain in robbery: if riches increase, do not set your heart upon them.'

We find that because they let pride come into their hearts, they eventually came under judgment.

Read Ezekiel 28:6-11,

> v. 6, 'Therefore this says the Lord God, Because you have set your heart as the heart of God;
>
> v. 7, Behold, therefore I will bring strangers upon you, the terrible of the nations: and they shall draw their swords against the beauty of your wisdom and they shall defile your brightness.
>
> v. 8, They shall bring you down to the pit and you shall die the deaths of them that are slain in the midst of the seas.
>
> v. 9, Will you yet say before him that slays you, I am God? But you shall be a man and no God, in the hand of him that slays you.

> v. 10, You shall die the deaths of the uncircumcised by the hand of strangers: for I have spoken it, says the Lord God.

God warns us many times that our increased wealth can become a snare to us.

Read Deut. 8:16-18,

> v. 16, 'Who fed you in the wilderness with manna, which your fathers knew not, that He might humble you and that He might prove you, to do you good at your latter end:
>
> v. 17, And you said in your heart, My power and the might of my hand has gotten me this wealth.'
>
> v. 18, But you shall remember the Lord your God: for it is He that gives you power to get wealth, that he may establish His covenant which He swore unto your fathers, as it is this day.'

Also look at 2 Timothy 3:1-9,

> v. 1, 'This know also, that in the last days perilous times shall come.
>
> v. 2, For men shall be lovers of their own selves, covetous, boasters, proud, blasphemers, disobedient to parents, unthankful, unholy,

v. 3, Without natural affection, truce-breakers, false accusers, incontinent, fierce, despisers of those that are good,

v. 4, Traitors, heady, high-minded, lovers of pleasures more than lovers of God;

v. 5, Having a form of godliness, but denying the power thereof: from such turn away.

v. 6, For of this sort are they which creep into houses and lead captive silly women laden with sins, led away with divers lusts,

v. 7, Ever learning and never able to come to the knowledge of the truth.

v. 8, Now as Jannes and Jambres withstood Moses, so do these also resist the truth: men of corrupt minds, reprobate concerning the faith.

v. 9, But they shall proceed no further for their folly shall be manifest to all men, as theirs also was.'

Lucifer himself was involved in some sort of traffic or merchandise.

The Hebrew word, "REKULLA", means trade, as peddled, to travel for trading, to go about for traffic as a dealer.

I believe this shows us another of his (Satan's) characteristics, such as in drug dealing. John 10:10, *'The thief comes not, but to steal and to kill and to destroy: I am come that they might have life and that they might have it more abundantly.'*

The word is used in the Old Testament when speaking of "traveling merchants" or "middle-men" buying and selling goods.

To apply this term to Lucifer indicates that he originally acted as a middle-angel between God and the other angels. His merchandise may have included instructions, wisdom and commands that came from God to him. He would have passed this onto the angels and the angels' communication he would have passed back to God.

James Beall in his book, "Let Us Make Man", says that Lucifer was God's merchant in the sense that he passed God's direction down to the angels and passed the angels worship up to God.

> In Ezekiel 28:16a it says, *'By the multitude of your merchandise they have filled the midst of you with violence and you have sinned...'*

We see by this verse that God may have been condemning not only the King of Tyre, but Satan, who motivated the King to sin.

With the multitude of things passing from God, through Lucifer to the angels and visa versa, we begin to understand the primary reason for Lucifer's fall. He began to covet all that God had, the control, the power, the worship and he no longer desired to be the middle-man (angel), he wanted it for himself.

Dakes and Bullinger say that Lucifer's traffic became a slandering of God to the angels in order to incite a rebellion.

The wisdom, perfection of beauty, being perfect in all his ways and the position of covering cherub, were all corrupted by the covetousness of his heart and caused him to rise up in pride.

A man called Feinberg, in a commentary on Ezekiel, writes this concerning Satan.

> "The author cannot follow those views which inject without support a foreign and false mythology, a legendary atmosphere of a hypothetical ideal personality. It cannot be conceded that Ezekiel was following a free imagination, which admittedly was not usual with him. Instead, he appeared to have the situation of his day in mind with his attention riveted upon the ruler of Tyre, the embodiment of the people's pride and godlessness. But as he viewed the thoughts and ways of that monarch, he clearly discerned behind him the motivation force and personality who was

impelling him in his opposition to God. In short, he saw the work and activity of Satan whom the king of Tyre was emulating in so many ways."

Recall the incident in Matthew 16:21-23, where Peter was rebuked by our Lord Jesus.

> *v. 21, 'From that time forth Jesus began to show to his disciples, how He must go unto Jerusalem and suffer many things of the elders and chief priests and scribes and be killed and be raised again the third day.*
>
> *v. 22, 'Then Peter took him and began to rebuke him, saying, Be it far from you, Lord: this shall not be done to You.*
>
> *v. 23, But he turned and said unto Peter, Get behind me Satan: you are an offence to me: for you do not savour the things that be of God, but those that be of men.'*

No sterner words were spoken to anyone in Christ's earthly ministry. However, He did not mean that Peter had somehow become Satan himself. He was indicating that the motivation behind Peter's opposition to His going to Calvary was none other than the Prince of Demons. It appears to be a similar situation here as with the King of Tyre and the King of Babylon.

It must be repeated that the one addressed was not an ideal man expelled from Eden, some mythological figure popularly known or another individual, but the same monarch with whom the chapter began. But behind him stood one with whom he was compared.

If Satan, who was far superior to Ithobal of Tyre, received just punishment for arrogating to himself divine prerogatives in the dateless past, then the ruler of Tyre could not escape the outcome of his defiance of the Lord. Because some interpreters are so willing to place this entire description on the human plane, they must surmise that the passage is full of oriental exaggeration. If these be taken to refer ultimately to Satan, they are eminently intelligible and in place.

We can see by the scriptures in Ezekiel, Satan is the sinister figure who stands behind the human king of Tyre.

The question is, what do we learn about Satan's original condition and characteristics out of these verses.

1. Satan had great wisdom and beauty. Satan stood at the Zenith of God's creatures, filled with wisdom and perfect in beauty.

Look at Ezekiel 28:12,
'Son of man take up a lamentation upon the king of Tyrus and say to him, This says the Lord God; You seal up the sum, full of wisdom and perfect in beauty.'

2. Satan's habitation. This may refer to a heavenly Eden or to the earthly Eden. In either case, it was before sin entered.

Read verse 13,

> 'You have been in Eden the garden of God; every precious stone was your covering, the sardius, topaz and the diamond, the beryl, the onyx and the jasper, the sapphire, the emerald and the carbuncle and gold: the workmanship of your tabrets and of your pipes was prepared in you in the day that you were created.'

3. Satan was a covering cherub. The dazzling description of his dress or robe indicates something of the glory bestowed on him. Satan was not satisfied with his beauty. It became corrupted by the covertness of his heart and caused him to rise in pride, v. 13.

4. Satan had a definite function. v. 14, 'You are the anointed cherub that covers; and I have set you so: you were upon the holy mountain of God; you have walked up and down in the midst of the stones of fire.'

He belonged to the order of angelic creatures designated, cherubim. They are associated with guarding:

- <u>The holiness of God.</u> Gen 3:24 says, 'So He drove out the man and he placed at the east of the garden of Eden, Cherubim and a flaming sword which turned every way, to keep the way of the tree of life.'

- **The throne of God.** Ezekiel 1:5 says, 'Also out of the midst thereof came the likeness of four living creatures and this was their appearance; they had the likeness of a man.'

- **The actual presence of God.** Satan was on the Holy Mountain of God, and he walked in the midst of the stones of fire, likely references to the presence of God Himself.

Apparently, Satan was the chief guardian of God's holiness and majesty. In his position, we can see that Satan had a will to do what was right or wrong. We can also see that Satan began to covet all that God had, the control, the power and the worship, and as we said, he no longer desired to be the middle-man.

Look at the example of Simon the Sorcerer in Acts 8:9-22.

5. Satan had unparalleled perfection. He was perfect in the sense of being completely sound and having total moral integrity. Look at verses 13 and 15.

Donald Grey Barnhouse wrote, "The Invisible War". In his writings he said this:

> "In every way, Satan was the epitome of God's creation. He awoke in the first moment of his existence in the full-orbed beauty and power of his exalted position; surrounded by all the magnif-

icence, which God gave him. He saw himself as above all the hosts in power, wisdom and beauty. Only at the throne of God itself did he see more than he himself possessed and it is possible that even that was in some sense not fully visible to the eyes of the creature."

Satan before his fall, it may be said, occupied the role of prime minister for God, ruling possibly over the universe, but certainly over this world.

Chapter Two

THE FALL OF LUCIFER

REVISION -

In Ezekiel 28:1-19, we found that there was a double reference to the person being addressed. The initial reference was to the Prince of Tyre, and the second reference was to Satan or Lucifer.

1. In the Scriptures, we found that when God was speaking concerning the King of Tyre, He was speaking of some leader of that city. History shows us that His name was Ithoblus.

2. We also found where God's judgment came upon the city.

3. We discovered that Satan was not created evil. He was created perfect or as some Bibles say, 'blameless'. Ezekiel 28:15 says, *'You were perfect in your ways from the day that you were created, till iniquity was found in you.'*

4. We learnt that because of his beauty, pride entered into his life. He wanted the things he didn't have, power, control and worship that belong to God and God only.

So now we will look into his fall in Isaiah 14:4-23. We find in Isaiah, it also has a double reference to the person being addressed. Firstly to the King of Babylon and then it refers to Lucifer. We shared on the King of Babylon.

In the last lesson, we found that Babylon is everything that opposes God. It is also pictured as the seat of evil. Read Revelation, chapters 17 and 18.

Babylon was permitted to bring corrections or havoc upon God's wayward children (Israel), but only to get them to turn back to God.

The Fall of Lucifer

Let us look at Isaiah 14:12-17,

> *v. 12, 'How are you fallen from heaven, O Lucifer, son of the morning! How are you cut down to the ground, which weakened the nations!*

> *v. 13, For you have said in your heart, I will ascend into heaven, I will exalt my throne above the stars of God: I will sit also upon the mount of the congregation, in the sides of the north;*

v. 14, I will ascend above the heights of the clouds; I will be like the most High.'

v. 15, Yet you shall be brought down to hell, to the sides of the pit.

v. 16, They that see you shall narrowly look upon you and consider you, saying, Is this the man that made the earth to tremble, that did shake kingdoms;

v. 17, That make the world as a wilderness and destroyed the cities thereof; that opened not the house of his prisoners?'

In these verses, there are several interpretations with regard to Satan as the fallen one.

1st Interpretation: He is Satan (Lucifer), because the person here is believed to be too powerful for any human King.

2nd Interpretation: This could be either Sennacherib or Nebuchadnezzar, Kings with supreme power. At that time, their people looked upon these kings as gods. History shows us and the Bible tells us that these kings wanted to rule the world. We know that Satan also wants to do this.

3rd Interpretation: This could refer to both Satan and a great human king, possibly Nebuchadnezzar, because

Babylon is pictured as the seat of evil in Revelation, chapters 17, 18.

Most scholars believe that this is a double reference concerning man and Satan.

Now, the five "I wills" of rebellion in Isaiah 14, verses 13 and 14.

1. 'I will ascend to heaven', means that Satan desired to occupy the same place as God in equal recognition. The creature wanted to expel the Creator. The servant wanted to be served.

> *v. 13, 'For you have said in your heart, I will ascend into heaven, I will exalt my throne above the stars of God: I will sit also upon the mount of the congregation, in the sides of the north.'*

2. 'I will raise my throne above the stars of God', expresses a desire for independent rule apart from God. In Job 38:7, we have a clue to the meaning of the phrase, 'the stars of God'.

This could refer to the heavenly bodies that illuminate the night. Most likely, it refers to Satan's desire to exalt himself to rule over the angelic kingdom of God.

> Job 38:7 says, "When the morning stars sang together and all the sons of God shouted for joy?"

3. 'I will sit on the mount of the Assembly in the recesses of the north', this describes Satan's ambition to control all the affairs of the universe. In other words, he wants Christ's position in the Kingdom.

Often in scripture, mountains and hills refer to authority or the right to rule. In Isaiah 2:2 it says, *'Now it will come about that in the last days, the mountain of the house of the Lord shall be established as the chief of the mountains and will be raised above the hills; & all the nations will stream to it.'*

This anticipates the Messiah's rule or Kingdom, called here, 'the mountain of the house of the Lord' and all the other kingdom's, mountain and hills, will be under His kingdom.

> Let's look at Psalm 48:2, *'Beautiful for situation the joy of the whole earth, is mount Zion, on the sides of the north, the city of the great King.'*

To sum up, Satan expressed his determination to rule over the affairs of the entire created universe.

4. 'I will ascend above the heights of the clouds.'

Isaiah 14:14 says,

> *v. 14, 'I will ascend above the heights of the clouds; I will be like the most High.'* Here Satan wants to take God's glory.

According to Exodus 16:10 and Rev. 19:1, clouds are often associated with God's glory and presence.

> Exodus 16:10 says, *'And it came to pass, as Aaron spoke to the whole congregation of the children of Israel, that they looked toward the wilderness and behold, the glory of the Lord appeared in the cloud.'*

> Rev. 19:1 says, *'And after these things I heard a great voice of many people in heaven, saying, Alleluia; Salvation, and glory and honour and power unto the Lord our God.'*

In this scripture, it clearly states that God alone has all the honour, glory and power due to Him.

This, 'I will' however, expressed Satan's desire to usurp the glory that belonged to God.

A writer named, Pentecost, writes, *'When Lucifer said, 'I will ascend above the heights of the clouds', he was saying, 'I will take to myself a greater glory than belongs to God Himself.'*

You will remember that Ezekiel described the beauty and the glory that belonged to Lucifer in terms of the sun shining on polished gems. But this glory that belonged to Lucifer was not inherently his, it was reflected glory, from God.

God, who is the author of glory and the all-glorious one, revealed His glory through the work that came from His hand.

Pentecost says, how insane the thinking of this one is, that he could add glory to the infinite glory of God. It suggests that there was a deficiency in the glory of God and that Lucifer could complete that which was lacking.

5. 'I will make myself like the Most High'. Isaiah 14:14, *'I will ascend above the heights of the clouds; I will be like the most High.'*

This is an interesting point; Satan's own thinking here, 'To become like God' was, first of all, to admit that He was not a god. He was only a created being, one created by the Creator.

The question here is, in what way then could a creature be like the Creator? In what way could he be like the Most High? He was the wisest of God's beings, yet he was not 'omniscient' (all-knowing). He did not know all things. He was the most powerful of all of God's created beings, yet he was not 'omnipotent' (all-powerful). He could go from one end of the created universe to another, but he was not 'omnipresent', (being everywhere, ever-present).

So in what way could he be like the most high? There was only one way. That was to be totally and completely independent of any authority outside of himself.

He could be like God only in being responsible to no one but himself. (To get rid of God is impossible.)

The desire of Satan was to move in and occupy the throne of God. Exercise absolute independent authority over the angelic creation, bring the earth and all the universe under his authority, cover himself with the glory that belongs to God alone and then be responsible to no one but himself.

The words, 'Most High' in the Hebrew are 'El-Elyon' and means, the possessor of heaven and earth.

To summarize, in all, Satan wants God's power and authority. He wants to remove God, be totally in control and receive worship and power.

So we can see through Isaiah 14:13,14 the factors that lead to Satan's downfall, which are summed up in the five "I wills" of rebellion.

In each of the five 'I wills', we find that Satan reveals not only his intentions, but also his agenda for as long as he is free to walk about the universe.

His intentions are always to cause man to love his kind of life rather than God's way of life. He wants man to be independent and therefore, not dependent on God.

He desires man to be in control of his own destiny and to receive worship so that man will think he is doing it in his own power.

Satan's first temptation was to get man to eat of the tree of good and evil that man might walk in independent rebellion; that man might be like God.

Genesis 3:5 says,

> V. 5, 'For God knows that in the day that you eat of it, then your eyes shall be opened and you shall be as gods, knowing good and evil.'

Still today, Satan is constantly seeking to reproduce this mentality in the saved and unsaved alike, and unfortunately, he finds willing targets.

1 Peter 5:8 says,

> v. 8 'Be sober, be vigilant; because your adversary the devil, as a roaring lion, walks about, seeking whom he may devour.'

For example, we have encounters, and their purpose is to allow God to pinpoint things in our lives, so that we can deal with them.

God wants us to be totally open with Him so we can become the leaders God desires us to be. Paul gives us an account of how we should and should not select leaders.

Let's read 1 Timothy 3:6,

> v. 6, 'Not a novice, lest being lifted up with pride he fall into the condemnation of the devil.'

It's easy for us to look at the gifts, abilities and opportunities God has given us and then like Satan, use these to bring glory to ourselves. Just as Satan's beauty and gifts are a reflection that came from God, we too need to remember that our gifts and knowledge also come from God.

Whatever we have is God given. Paul warned that when selecting elders, a novice should not be selected. Why is this? Because he will fall into pride. The result of this being, he will fall under condemnation incurred by the devil.

We have looked at Satan's origin, the beginnings of his existence and his fall. Now we will look at other scriptures concerning the existence of Satan and his demons in the Old and New Testaments.

Firstly we will look at Psalm 106:34 – 37,

> *v. 34, 'They did not destroy the nations, concerning whom the Lord commanded them:*
>
> *v. 35, But were mingled among the heathen and learned their works.*
>
> *v. 36, And they served their idols which were a snare to them.*
>
> *v. 37, Yes they sacrifice their sons and their daughters to devils.*

Israel was told to rid themselves of the wickedness from within the land and from within the people in it.

Israel constantly turned away from God. In their time, they saw miracles from God, but still turned from Him to worship the idols of the land (verse 36).

Most of us have seen miracles and provision from God, but we can also be enticed by the world's gods. For example, power, fame, sex, pleasure and materialism. We need to remember all that God has done for us so that we won't be drawn away to follow after the lusts of the flesh and demons.

Look at 1 Timothy 4:1,

> v. 1, 'Now the Spirit speaks expressly, that in the latter times some shall depart from the faith, giving heed to seducing spirits and doctrines of devils.'

Secondly, Psalm 109:6 talks about an evil man to oppose him and letting the accuser stand at his right hand.

> v. 6, 'You set a wicked man over him and let Satan stand at this right hand.'

Satan is recognized as the accuser, and we will see more of this when we discuss the other names he has.

Satan is recognized as a liar in John 8:44,

> v. 44, 'You are of your father the devil, and the lusts of your father you will do. He was a murderer from the beginning and does not abide in the truth, because the truth is not in him. When he speaks a lie, he speaks of his own: for he is a liar and the father of it.'

Jesus also mentioned Satan in Luke 10:18. Jesus saw him fall like lightning.

> v. 18, 'And He (the Lord) said to them, I beheld Satan as lightning fall from heaven.'

So, we have seen that there is much proof of Satan's existence. In the Bible, there are twenty-nine references to him in the Gospels alone. Also in nineteen of the twenty-seven books of the New Testament, Satan is mentioned.

Chapter Three

The Personality of Satan

The Traits of Personality

Like the angels, Satan also is said to possess the traits of personality.

1. He shows intelligence.

2 Corinthians 11:3, 4 says,

> v. 3, 'But I am afraid that just as Eve was deceived by the serpent's cunning, your minds may somehow be led astray from your sincere and pure devotion to Christ.
>
> v. 4, For if someone comes to you and preaches a Jesus other than the Jesus we preached, or if you receive a different spirit from the one you received,

or a different gospel from the one you accepted, you put up with it easily enough.'

The Corinthian believers fell for smooth talk and messages that sounded good and seemed to make sense. This is similar to Eve, when Satan deceived her at the Fall, using his knowledge for deception.

2. He exhibits emotions.

Revelation 12:17 says,

> v. 7, 'Then the dragon was enraged at the woman and went off to make war against the rest of her offspring; those who obey God's commandments and hold to the testimony of Jesus.'

Satan was **enraged and angered.** The apostle John, here in verse 17, shows us the war is still being waged, but the outcome has already been determined. Satan and his followers have been defeated and will be destroyed.

In Ephesians 6:10-12, Paul shows us that we too are in a spiritual battle.

> v. 10, 'Finally, be strong in the Lord and in his mighty power.

> v. 11, Put on the full armour of God so that you can take your stand against the devil's schemes.

> v. 12, For our struggle is not against flesh and blood, but against the rulers, against the authorities, against the powers of this dark world and against the spiritual forces of evil in the heavenly realms.'

Never the less, Satan is battling daily to bring more into his ranks and to keep his own from defecting to God's side.

The good news is that those who belong to Christ have gone into battle on God's side, and He has guaranteed us victory.

We can see in Satan's emotion, that he is enraged. God will not lose the war, but we must make certain not to lose the battle of our souls. We need not waver in our commitment to Christ. There is a great spiritual battle being fought, and there is not the time for indecision.

3. Satan has a desire.

Luke 22:31,32 says,

> v. 31, 'Simon, Simon, Satan has asked to sift you as wheat.

> v. 32, But I have prayed for you, Simon, that your faith may not fail. And when you have turned back, strengthen your brothers.'

Satan had a desire to sift Peter. Satan wanted to crush Peter and the other disciples like grains of wheat. He hoped to find chaff and blow it away. This is what Satan hopes to find in us, and he hopes to blow us away also.

Jesus assured Peter that his faith, although it would falter, would not be destroyed. Notice in verse 32, Jesus prayed for Peter. How much more we should do the same for each other. Jesus prayed that Peter's faith would not be destroyed, it would be renewed, and Peter, in the end, would become a powerful leader.

4. Satan has a will.

Isaiah 14:12-14 says,

> *v. 12, 'How you have fallen from heaven, O Lucifer, O morning star, son of the morning! You have been cast down to the earth, you who once laid low the nations.*

> *v. 13, For you have said in your heart, I will ascend into heaven, I will exalt my throne above the stars of God: I will sit also upon the mount of the congregation, in the sides of the north;*

> *v. 14, I will ascend above the heights of the clouds; I will be like the Most High.'*

We found in the five 'I wills' of Satan that he only exposes his intention, which is to get man to live his kind of life and not God's way of life.

Look at 2 Timothy 2:26,

> v. 26, 'And that they will come to their senses and escape from the trap of the devil, who has taken them captive to do his will.'

We can see by these traits we find, the devil is a created angel. Satan is held responsible for his actions. He was not merely a personification that people have devised to express their ideas of evil; he is a person with a will and emotions, desires and intellect. Satan is held accountable to the Lord.

Matthew 25:41 says,

> v. 41, 'Then He (the Lord) will say to those on his left, Depart from me, you who are cursed, into the eternal fire prepared for the devil and his angels.'

Chapter Four

Specific Names Applied to Satan

Let us look at some of the names that Satan has been connected with and what they mean.

1. Satan.

Job 1:6-9 says,

> v. 6, 'One day the angels came to present themselves before the Lord and Satan also came with them.
>
> v. 7, The Lord said to Satan, Where have you come from? Satan answered the Lord, From roaming through the earth and going back and forth in it.
>
> v. 8, Then the Lord said to Satan, Have you considered my servant Job? There is no one on earth like

him; he is blameless and upright, a man who fears God and shuns evil.

v. 9, Does Job fear God for nothing?, Satan replied.'

Matthew 4:10 says,

v. 10, 'Jesus said to him, Away from me Satan. For it is written: Worship the Lord your God, and serve Him only.'

The title "Satan" occurs 53 times in 47 verses in the Bible. The Greek word is "Satanas", and the Hebrew is "sAa,Lan". The primary idea is: adversary, one who withstands. It points to Satan as the opponent of God, of believers and all that is right and good.

We should note however, that Satan often appears as an angel of light, promising what is supposed to be good.

Genesis 3:1 says,

v. 1, 'Now the serpent was more crafty than any of the wild animals the Lord God had made. He said to the woman, Did God really say, You must not eat from any tree in the garden?'

We can also see that Satan and his servants can deceive us by appearing to be attractive, good and moral.

SPECIFIC NAMES APPLIED TO SATAN

The Bible shows us that many unsuspecting people follow smooth-talking, Bible-quoting leaders into cults that alienate them from their families and lead them into the practice of immorality and deceit. How do we check out these deceivers?

a) Check to see if the teaching is confirmed by Scriptures.

Acts 17:11 says,

> v. 11, 'Now the Bereans were of more noble character than the Thessalonians, for they received the message with great eagerness and examined the Scriptures every day to see if what Paul said was true.'

b) Does the teacher affirm and proclaim that Jesus Christ is God Who came into the world as a man to save people from their sins?

1 John 4:1-3 says,

> v. 1, 'Dear friends, do not believe every spirit, but test the spirits to see whether they are from God, because many false prophets have gone out into the world.
>
> v. 2, This is how you can recognise the Spirit of God: Every spirit that acknowledges that Jesus Christ has come in the flesh is from God,

v. 3, But every spirit that does not acknowledge Jesus, is not from God. This is the spirit of the Antichrist, which you have heard is coming and even now is already in the world.'

c) Is the teacher's lifestyle consistent with Biblical morality?

Matthew 12:33-37 says,

v. 33, 'Make a tree good and its fruit will be good, or make a tree bad and its fruit will be bad, for a tree is recognized by its fruit.

v. 34, You brood of vipers, how can you who are evil say anything good? For out of the overflow of the heart the mouth speaks.

v. 35, The good man brings good things our of the good stored up in him and the evil man brings evil things out of the evil stored up in him.

v. 36, But I tell you that men will have to give account on the day of judgement for every careless word they have spoken.

v. 37, For by your words you will be acquitted and by your words you will be condemned.'

To conclude, the name 'Satan' means adversary or

SPECIFIC NAMES APPLIED TO SATAN

opposing one who takes a stand against God and man's well being.

Zechariah 3:1 says,

> v. 1, 'Then He showed me Joshua the high priest standing before the angel of the Lord and Satan standing at his right side to accuse him.'

Revelation 12:9 says,

> v. 9, 'The great dragon was hurled down; that ancient serpent called the devil, or Satan, who leads the whole world astray. He was hurled to the earth and his angels with him.'

2. The Devil.

Matthew 4:1,5,9 says,

> v. 1, 'Then Jesus was lead by the spirit into the desert to be tempted by the devil.
>
> v. 5, Then the devil took Him to the holy city and had Him stand on the highest point to the temple.
>
> v. 9, All this I will give you, he said, if you will bow down and worship me.'

Ephesians 4:27 says,

> v. 27, 'And do not give the Devil a foothold.'

Revelation 20:2 says,

> v. 2, 'He seized the dragon, that ancient serpent, who is the devil, or Satan, and bound him for a thousand years.'

Devil in the Greek is: "diabolos" which means, slander, or one trips up (de Famer).

1 Peter 5:8 says,

> v. 8, 'Be self-controlled and alert. Your enemy the devil prowls around like a roaring lion looking for someone to devour.'

This shows us that the devil is looking around to see who he can trip up (devour).

Lions attack sick, young or straggling animals. They choose victims who are alone or not alert.

Peter warns us to watch out for Satan when we are suffering or being persecuted. There are times when we are feeling alone, weak, helpless and cut off from other believers, so focused on our troubles that we forget to watch for danger.

SPECIFIC NAMES APPLIED TO SATAN

We are especially vulnerable to Satan's attacks. During times of suffering, we need to seek other Christians for support.

We need to keep our eyes on Christ, resist the devil and he will flee from us.

James 4:7 says,

> v. 7, 'Submit yourselves then to God. Resist the Devil and he will flee from you.'

To conclude with the name "devil", it can be said that he is the one who slanders God to man.

Genesis 3:1-7 says,

> v. 1, 'Now the serpent was more crafty than any of the wild animals the Lord God had made. He said to the woman, Did God really say, You must not eat from any tree in the garden?'

> v. 2, The woman said to the serpent, We may eat fruit from the trees in the garden

> v. 3, But God did say, You must not eat fruit from the tree that is in the middle of the garden and you must not touch it, or you will die.

> v. 4, *You will not surely die, the serpent said to the woman.*
>
> v. 5, *For God knows that when you eat of it, your eyes will be opened and you will be like God, knowing good and evil.*
>
> v. 6, *When the woman saw that the fruit of the tree was good for food and pleasing to the eye, and also desirable for gaining wisdom, she took some and ate it. She also gave some to her husband, who was with her, and he ate it.*
>
> v. 7, *Then the eyes of both of them were opened and they realized they were naked; so they sewed fig leaves together and made coverings for themselves.'*

And he also slanders man to God.

Job 1:9 and 2:4 says,

> v. 9, *'Does Job fear God for nothing? Satan replied.'*
>
> v. 4, *'Skin for skin!, Satan replied. A man will give all he has for his own life.'*

SPECIFIC NAMES APPLIED TO SATAN

3. Old Serpent.

Revelation 12:9 says,

> v. 9, 'The great dragon was hurled down; that ancient serpent called the devil, or Satan, who leads the whole world astray. He was hurled to the earth and his angels with him.'

This name for Satan looks back to the account in Genesis 3 and the temptation in the garden. It is designed to remind us of his crafty deception and guile.

2 Corinthians 11:3 says,

> v. 3, 'But I fear, lest by any means, as the serpent beguiled Eve through his subtlety, so your minds should be corrupted from the simplicity that is in Christ.'

The word 'old' indicates that he has been around a long time and is well known.

4. Lucifer.

Isaiah 14:12 says,

> v. 12, 'How you have fallen from heaven, O morning star, son of the dawn! You have been cast down to the earth, you who once laid low the nations!'

Lucifer means, "Son of the Morning", also "shining one" and "son of the dawn".

The Hebrew word for Lucifer is "helel", literally, "the shining one." It means, "to shine" or it can mean, "to boast or praise", anyway, the shining one took his eyes off the Lord, the source of his brilliance, becoming proud and boastful instead of being full of praise for God's glory.

He became prideful and forgot that he only had the reflected glory of God. He was the created one, not the Creator.

5. The Dragon.

Revelation 12:3,7,9 says,

> *v. 3, 'Than another sign appeared in heaven: an enormous red dragon with seven heads and ten horns and seven crowns on his heads.*
>
> *v. 7, And there was war in heaven. Michael and his angels fought against the dragon, and the dragon and his angels fought back.*
>
> *v. 9, The great dragon was hurled down; that ancient serpent called the devil, or Satan, who leads the whole world astray. He was hurled to the earth and his angels with him.'*

Great dragon means, "serpent" or "sea monster". The word is used to express the ruthless aggression with which Satan seeks to oppress people. He is cruel and vicious. This name is especially related to his end-time character and world system when God removes all restraints and allows him to go his natural way, to become what he naturally is.

Look at John 8:44 says,

> v. 44, 'You belong to your father, the Devil and you want to carry out your father's desire. He was a murderer from the beginning, not holding to the truth, for there is no truth in him. When he lies, he speaks his native language, for he is a liar and the father of lies.'

6. The Prince of the Power of the Air.

Ephesians 2:2 says,

> v. 22, 'In which you used to live when you followed the ways of the world and of the ruler of the kingdom of the air, the spirit who is now at work in those who are disobedient.'

This points to Satan as the head of the demonic hosts, meaning he is the ruler of those spiritual beings of the kingdom of darkness that inhabit the atmosphere surrounding the earth.

Though the word, "power" is singular, many scholars or commentaries believe it refers to the demonic forces as a corporate body, all of whom operate as one organized body under Satan, their ruler.

Look at Ephesians 6:12 says,

> v. 12, 'For our struggle is not against flesh and blood, but against the rulers, against the authorities, against the powers of this dark world and against the spiritual forces of evil in the heavenly realms.'

The word, 'air' in the Greek is "Ahr" meaning, atmosphere.

7. The Evil One.

1 John 5:19 says,

> v. 19, 'And we know that we are of God and the whole world lies in wickedness.'

Satan is described as, "the Evil One", meaning:

- Wicked
- Sinful
- Worthless
- Bad
- Vicious
- Degenerate

SPECIFIC NAMES APPLIED TO SATAN

While most translations have, "the Evil One", the King James translates it only as "the Evil".

The 'Evil One' points to Satan's character. He is actively engaged in destruction, by causing:

- Pain
- Injury
- Death

He is cancer to the human race, meaning that corruption spreads uncontrollably.

8. The God of this World or Age.

2 Corinthians 4:4 says,

> 'The god of this world has blinded the minds of unbelievers, so that they cannot see the light of the gospel of the glory of Christ, who is the image of God.'

The meaning of this, is believed to be Satan's rulership over the economy, which is marked by a growing increase in apostasy, deception and moral decay.

In Galatians 1:4, Paul calls this, "the present EVIL Age". The point here is that Satan is the reason this age will never improve, because it takes its character from Satan, the evil one. It is the Evil Age that grows worse because of his presence and activity to both undermine the plan of God and set up his own rule and worship, as seen in Revelation 13.

Galatians 1:4 says,

> v. 4, 'Who gave himself for our sins to rescue us from the present evil age, according to the will of our God and Father.'

We can see that in this verse, it shows us we walk according to the world governed by the philosophy of Satan and his demonic forces. We have to sift out what is good. "Age" in the Greek is "AION". It means, a system or a course of philosophy by which one governs one's life.

9. The Prince of Demons.

This is Beelzebub, a heathen god believed to be the ruler of all demons.

Matthew 12:24 says,

> v. 15, 'But when the Pharisees heard this, they said, It is only by Beelzebub, the prince of demons, that this fellow drives out demons.'

Luke 11:15 says,

> v. 24, 'But some of them said, By Beelzebub, the prince of demons, he is driving out demons.'

SPECIFIC NAMES APPLIED TO SATAN

2 Kings 1:2,3,6,16 says,

v. 2, 'Now Ahaziah had fallen through the lattice of his upper room in Samaria and injured himself. So he sent messengers, saying to them, Go and consult Baal-Zebub, the god of Ekron, to see if I will recover from this injury.

v. 3, But the angel of the Lord said to Elijah the Tishbite, Go up and meet the messengers of the king of Samaria and ask them, Is it because there is no God in Israel that you are going off to consult Baal-Zebub, the god of Ekron?

v. 6, A man came to meet us, they replied. And he said to us, God back to the king who sent you and tell him, this is what the Lord says: Is it because there is no God in Israel that you are sending men to consult Baal-Zebub, the god of Ekron? Therefore you will not leave the bed you are lying on. You will certainly die!

v. 16, He told the king, This is what the Lord says: Is it because there is no God in Israel for you to consult that you have sent messengers to consult Baal-Zebub, the god of Ekron? Because you have done this, you will never leave the bed you are lying on. You will certainly die!'

He was the god Ekron, and from the Scripture references, it was believed to have the power to know the future.

The Pharisees had already accused Jesus of being in league with the prince of demons.

Look at Matthew 9:34 says,

> v.34, 'But the Pharisees said, It is by the prince of demons that he drives out demons.'

The Pharisees were trying to discredit Jesus by using an emotional argument. They refused to believe that Jesus came from God. They said He was in league with Satan.

10. The Destroyer.

Revelation 9:11 says,

> v. 11, 'They had as king over them the angel of the Abyss, whose name in Hebrew is Abaddon, and in Greek, Apollyon.'

Abaddon is the Hebrew form, and Apollyon is the Greek equivalent. Both of these words mean: destroyer, destruction.

The name connects Satan as the head over the Demons of the Abyss and their work of destruction that will occur when he is given the key to the abyss in the tribulation and releases these demon hordes on the people of the earth.

Primarily, however, this title stresses his work of destruction.

Satan works to destroy the glory of God and God's purpose with man. Satan works to destroy societies and mankind. In all this, we can see his hatred for man and his desire to inflict pain upon man without regard for the person. **We must remember** Satan has no good side.

11. The Tempter

Matthew 4:3 says,

> v. 3, 'The tempter came to him and said, If you are the Son of God, tell these stones to become bread.'

1 Thessalonians 3:5 says,

> v. 5, 'For this reason, when I could stand it no longer, I sent to find out about your faith. I was afraid that in some way the tempter might have tempted you and our efforts might have been useless.'

Paul warns about being tempted in marriage.

1 Corinthians 7:5 says,

> v. 5, 'Do not deprive each other except by mutual consent and for a time, so that you may devote

yourselves to prayer. Then come together again so that Satan will not tempt you because of your lack of self-control.'

Satan relies on:

a) His network of demons to tempt.

The tempter is of the devil, but can't do all the tempting. Satan is not omnipresent, but he is the ultimate source of temptation. Satan must rely on his agents to carry out his temptation.

b) The world system, which relies on his control.

1 John 5:19 says,

> v. 19, 'We know that we are children of God and that the whole world is under the control of the evil one.'

c) The carnality of ignorant Christians. He is able to use Christians as he did Peter.

Matthew 16:22-23 says,

> v. 22, 'Peter took him aside and began to rebuke Him. Never Lord, he said. This shall never happen to you!.

v. 23, Jesus turned and said to Peter, Get behind me, Satan! You are a stumbling block to Me; you do not have in mind the things of God, but the things of men.'

d) Unbelievers under his influence or domination.

Luke 22:1-6 says,

v. 1, 'Now the Feast of Unleavened Bread, called the Passover, was approaching,

v. 2 And the chief priests and the teachers of the law were looking for some way to get rid of Jesus, for they were afraid of the people.

v. 3, Then Satan entered Judas, called Iscariot, one of the Twelve.

v. 4, And Judas went to the chief priests and the officers of the temple guard and discussed with them how he might betray Jesus.

v. 5, They were delighted and agreed to give him money.

v. 6, He consented and watched for an opportunity to hand Jesus over to them when no crowd was present.'

Ephesians 2:2 says,

> v. 2, 'In which you used to live when you followed the ways of this world and of the ruler of the kingdom of the air, the spirit who is now at work in those who are disobedient.'

Satan's agencies:

The three primary avenues of his temptation are:

1. Lusts of the flesh.
2. Lusts of the eyes.
3. The pride of life.

1 John 2:16 says,

> v. 16, 'For everything in the world, the craving of sinful man, the lust of the eyes and the boasting of what he has and does, comes not from the Father but for the world.'

The processes Satan uses:

Satan uses people to make negative choices against God; for example, Peter.

Matthew 16:22,23 says,

> v. 22, 'Peter took him aside and began to rebuke

Him. Never Lord, he said. This shall never happen to you!.

v. 23, Jesus turned and said to Peter, Get behind me, Satan! You are a stumbling block to Me; you do not have in mind the things of God, but the things of men.'

We must avoid setting ourselves up for temptation.

Proverbs 7: 6-10 says,

v. 6, 'For at the window of my house I looked out through my lattice,

v. 7, And I saw among the naïve, I discerned among the youths, a young man lacking sense,

v. 8, Passing through the street near her corner; And he takes the way to her house,

v. 9, In the twilight, in the evening in the middle of the night and in the darkness

v. 10, And behold, a woman comes to meet him, dressed as a harlot and cunning of heart.'

This Scripture shows us that our heart, our feelings of love and desire, dictate to a great extent how we live; because we always find time to do what we enjoy.

Solomon tells us to guard our heart above all else. We need to concentrate on our desires that will keep us on the right path. It says in 2 Corinthians 10:5,

> v. 5, 'We demolish arguments and every pretension that sets itself up against the knowledge of God and we take captive every thought to make it obedient to Christ.'

Philippians 4:8 says,

> v. 8, 'Finally brothers, whatever is noble, whatever is right, whatever is pure, whatever is lovely, whatever is admirable, if anything is excellent or praiseworthy, think about such things.'

James 1:12-15 says,

> v. 12, 'Blessed is the man who preservers under trial, because when he has stood the test, he will receive the crown of life that God has promised to those who love Him.

> v. 13, When tempted, no one should say, God is tempting me. For God cannot be tempted by evil, nor does He tempt anyone;

SPECIFIC NAMES APPLIED TO SATAN

> *v. 14, But each is tempted when, by his own evil desires, he is dragged away and enticed.*

> *v. 15, Then after desire has conceived, it gives birth to sin; and sin, when it is full-grown, gives birth to death.'*

When we are tempted, we should have our armour on.

The armour of the Believer:

a) Resist the devil by drawing near and putting on the full armour of God.

James 4:7 says,

> *v. 7, 'Submit yourselves then to God. Resist the devil and he will flee from you.*

1 Peter 5:9 says,

> *v. 9, 'Resist him, standing firm in the faith, because you know that your brothers throughout the world are undergoing the same kind of sufferings.'*

Ephesians 6:13 says,

> *v. 13, 'Therefore put on the full armour of God, so that when the day of evil comes, you may be able to stand your ground, and after you have done everything, to stand.'*

b) Run or flee temptation, avoid unnecessary places or conditions.

2 Timothy 2:22 says,

> v. 22, 'Flee the evil desires of youth and pursue righteousness, faith, love and peace, along with those who call on the Lord out of a pure heart.'

Proverbs 5:8 says,

> v. 8, 'Keep to a path fat from her, do not go near the door of her house…'

Proverbs 7:6-10 says,

> v. 6, 'For at the window of my house I looked out through my lattice,

> v. 7, And I saw among the naïve, I discerned among the youths, a young man lacking sense,

> v. 8, Passing through the street near her corner; And he takes the way to her house,

> v. 9, In the twilight, in the evening in the middle of the night and in the darkness

> v. 10, And behold, a woman comes to meet him, dressed as a harlot and cunning of heart.'

SPECIFIC NAMES APPLIED TO SATAN

c) Render marital rights in marriage.

1 Corinthians 7:1-5 says,

> v. 1, 'Now concerning the things about which you wrote, it is good for a man not to touch a woman.
>
> v. 2, But because of immoralities, let each man have his own wife and let each woman have her own husband.
>
> v. 3, Let the husband fulfil his duty to his wife and likewise also the wife to her husband.'
>
> v. 4, The wife does not have authority over her own body, but the husband does; and likewise also the husband does not have authority over his own body, but the wife does.
>
> v. 5, Stop depriving one another, except by agreement for a time that you may devote yourselves to prayer and come together again lest Satan tempt you because of your lack of self control.'

d) Renew the mind, having a word filled life.

Romans 12:1-2 says,
> v. 1, 'Therefore, I urge you, brothers, in view of

God's mercy, to offer your bodies as living sacrifices, holy and pleasing to God, this is your spiritual act of worship.

v. 2, Do not conform any longer to the pattern of this world, but be transformed by the renewing of your mind. That you will be able to test and approve what God's will is, his good, pleasing and perfect will.'

Jesus was an example of a Word filled life.

Matthew 4:1-11 says,

v. 1, 'Then Jesus was led by the Spirit into the desert to be tempted by the devil.

v. 2, After fasting forty days and forty nights, he was hungry.

v. 3, The tempter came to Him and said, If you are the Son of God, tell these stones to become bread.

v. 4, Jesus answered, It is written: Man does not live on bread alone, but on every word that comes from the mouth of God.

v. 5, Then the devil took Him to the Holy city and had him stand on the highest point of the temple.

SPECIFIC NAMES APPLIED TO SATAN

v. 6, If you are the Son of God, he said, Throw yourself down. For it is written: He will command His angels concerning you and they will lift you up in their hands, so that you will not strike your foot against a stone.

v. 7, Jesus answered him, it is also written: Do not put the Lord your God to the test.

v. 8, Again, the devil took Him to a very high mountain and showed Him all the kingdoms of the world and their splendour.

v. 9, All this I will give you, he said, if you will bow down and worship me.

v. 10, Jesus said to him, Away from me, Satan! For it is written: Worship the Lord your God and serve Him only.
v. 11, Then the devil left Him and angels came and attended Him.'

The word enables us to meet temptation head on and causes Satan to flee.

James 4:7 says,

v. 7, 'Submit yourselves, then, to God. Resist the devil and he will flee from you.'

12. Beelzebul.

Matthew 12:24 says,

> *v. 24 'But when the Pharisees heard this, they said, It is only by Beelzebub, the prince of demons, that this fellow drives out demons.'*

Mark 3:22 says,

> *v. 22, 'And the teachers of the law who came down from Jerusalem said, He is possessed by Beelzebub! By the prince of demons, He is driving out demons.'*

1st meaning: Beelzebub, "Lord of the dung". A name of reproach.

2nd meaning: Beelzebub, "Lord of the Flies". Either one of these are names of reproach and are names of uncleanliness applied to Satan. He is the prince of Demons and unclean.

3rd meaning: Beelzeboul, "The Lord of dwelling". This identifies Satan as the god of unclean spirits of demon possession. Need to take hold of the strong man.
Look at Matthew 10:25 says,

> *v. 25, 'It is enough for the student to be like his teacher, and the servant like his master. If the*

SPECIFIC NAMES APPLIED TO SATAN

head of the house has been called Beelzebub, how much more the members of this household!'

Matthew 12:29 says,

v. 29, 'Or again, how can anyone enter a strong man's house and carry off his possessions unless he first ties up the strong man? Then he can rob his house.'

KNOWING YOUR ENEMY

Chapter Five

The Origin of Demons

There are three primary views as to where demons came from:

1. They are a class of angel that fell with Satan at his rebellion. We must remember that Satan and demons are fallen beings and were created. In Ezekiel 28:15 it says, 'You were perfect in all your ways from the day you were created.'

We can see here that the Bible is talking about a created being, not a human being.

Lucifer had a throne of some type, because he said, "I will exalt my throne above the stars of God.'

Isaiah 14:13 says,
'You said in your heart, I will ascend to heaven; I will raise my throne above the stars of God; I will

sit enthroned on the mount of assembly, on the utmost heights of the sacred mountain.'

It's also believed that Satan had a type of kingdom on earth. This would lead us to believe in a pre-adamic race (pre-creation). Possibly there was some kind of kingdom on earth before man was created. Some scholars believe that millions of years may have come and gone between Genesis 1:1 and Genesis 1:2, which brings us to our second theory.

2. They are disembodied spirits of a pre-adamic race or creation, which was destroyed when Satan and his angels rebelled against God.

Genesis tells us that the earth was without form and darkness covered the face of the deep, and the Spirit of God moved upon the face of the waters.

Evidently, the spirits that are here on earth were part of that kingdom. God told Adam and Eve to go and replenish the earth, which means that life must have been here.

Replenish means:
1. To occupy a place as inhabitants or settlers.
2. To fill a place or space with something.

The Bible shows us that Lucifer has a kingdom here. Evil spirits are here on the earth. The question is, where did they come from? Evidently, there was a creation of some kind here on earth prior to Adam and Eve.

3. They are spirits of the unnatural offspring of the sons of God and the daughters of men. Genesis 6.

The difference between fallen angels and demons is that angels have the ability to take on human form, whereas a demon seeks to inhabit a human body.

In Mark 5:1-20, we read the story of a mad man in which demons inhabited a human body. When they were cast out of the body, they still wanted to go into another body. They were sent into the pigs, which expresses their personality. The man was naked, which shows his uncleanliness, and we know that pigs are considered unclean animals.

We find that the devil works through our flesh, whereas God works through our spirit.

After Adam and Eve fell, Adam sold out to the devil, who then became the god of this world.

2 Corinthians 4:4 says,

> v. 4, 'The god of this age has blinded the minds of unbelievers, so that they cannot see the light of the gospel of the glory of Christ, who is the image of God.'

KNOWING YOUR ENEMY

Chapter Six

Satan's Present Power and Activity

֍ ֎

Satan generates his power in four major area's.

1. In Relation to God.

Satan blinds men to the true light of God and turns their eyes to other things he sets about to counterfeit the truths of God in the church. Satan brings new enlightenments into the church.

a) Satan promotes false doctrine.

False teachers are still a threat to the church, so we should always be aware of what is being taught. Jesus and the apostles repeatedly warned us.

For example in 1 Timothy 4:1-3 it says,
> v. 1, 'The Spirit clearly says that in later times some will abandon the faith and follow deceiving spirits and things taught by demons.

v. 2, Such teachings come through hypocritical liars, whose consciences have been scared, as with a hot iron.

v. 3, They forbid people to marry and order them to abstain from certain foods, which God created to be received with thanksgiving by those who believe and who know the truth.'

Mark 13:21-23 says,

v. 21, 'At that time if anyone says to you, 'Look, here is the Christ!' or, 'Look, there he is!' do not believe it.

v. 22, For false Christs and false prophets will appear and perform signs and miracles to deceive the elect--if that were possible.

v. 23, So be on your guard; I have told you everything ahead of time.'

Acts 20:28-31 says,

v. 28, Keep watch over yourselves and all the flock of which the Holy Spirit has made you overseers. Be shepherds of the church of God, which he bought with his own blood.

v. 29, I know that after I leave, savage wolves will come in among you and will not spare the flock.

v. 30, Even from your own number men will arise and distort the truth in order to draw away disciples after them.

v. 31, So be on your guard! Remember that for three years I never stopped warning each of you night and day with tears.

2 Peter 3:3-7 says,

v. 3, 'First of all, you must understand that in the last days scoffers will come, scoffing and following their own evil desires.

v. 4, They will say, "Where is this 'coming' he promised? Ever since our fathers died, everything goes on as it has since the beginning of creation."

v. 5, But they deliberately forget that long ago by God's word the heavens existed and the earth was formed out of water and by water.

v. 6, By these waters also the world of that time was deluged and destroyed.

> v. 7, *By the same word the present heavens and earth are reserved for fire, being kept for the day of 'judgment and destruction of ungodly men.*

b) He sets out to counterfeit the power of Christ.

1 John 2:26-27 says,

> v. 26, *'I am writing these things to you about those who are trying to lead you astray.*

> v. 27, *As for you, the anointing you received from him remains in you, and you do not need anyone to teach you. But as his anointing teaches you about all things and as that anointing is real, not counterfeit--just as it has taught you, remain in him.'*

Here, we have the Holy Spirit within, then the anointing to keep us from going astray; in addition, we have God inspired Scripture by which we can test questionable teachings.

Satan will always use religion as a means to oppose God.

2. In Relation to the Nations.

Satan is the drawing force behind many Government powers.

SATAN'S PRESENT POWER AND ACTIVITY

2 Corinthians 4:4 says,

> v. 4, 'The god of this age has blinded the minds of unbelievers, so that they cannot see the light of the gospel of the glory of Christ, who is the image of God.'

This implies Satan's rulership over the economy, which is marked by a growing apostasy (turning from the truth), deception and moral decay.

3. In Relation to the Unsaved.

These people followed Jesus while He was teaching but didn't do anything about it, because Satan is always seeking to prevent people from accepting the Gospel.

For example it says in Luke 8: 12,

> v. 12, 'Those along the path are the ones who hear, and then the devil comes and takes away the word from their hearts, so that they may not believe and be saved.

4. In Relation to Christians.

James 4:7 says,

> v. 7, 'Submit yourselves, then, to God. Resist the devil and he will flee from you.'

KNOWING YOUR ENEMY

Christians are to seek Christ and submit to Him, to resist his attack.

Satan is trying to win us over to his evil ways. However, with the Holy Spirit's power, we can resist the devil and he will flee.

Matthew 16:23 says,

> *v. 23, Jesus turned and said to Peter, "Get behind me, Satan! You are a stumbling block to me; you do not have in mind the things of God, but the things of men."*

The devil seeks to use members against members and seeks to destroy one another. Satan is always trying to get God out of the picture – to defer from God's will.

Matthew 6:23 says,

> *v. 23, 'But if your eyes are bad, your whole body will be full of darkness. If then, the light within you is darkness, how great is that darkness!'*

Spiritual vision is our capacity to see clearly what God wants us to do, and also to see the world from His point of view. Our self-serving desires and interests, however, can easily cloud this viewpoint.

Just as the song, whose words reflect our need to look to Jesus and in doing so, everything else will grow dim.

The Church is in Warfare/Battle:

Ephesians 6:10-18 says,

> v. 10, 'Finally, be strong in the Lord and in his mighty power.
>
> v. 11, Put on the full armour of God so that you can take your stand against the devil's schemes.
>
> v. 12, For our struggle is not against flesh and blood, but against the rulers, against the authorities, against the powers of this dark world and against the spiritual forces of evil in the heavenly realms.
>
> v. 13, Therefore put on the full armour of God, so that when the day of evil comes, you may be able to stand your ground, and after you have done everything, to stand.
>
> v. 14, Stand firm then, with the belt of truth buckled around your waist, with the breastplate of righteousness in place.
>
> v. 15, And with your feet fitted with the readiness that comes from the gospel of peace.

v. 16 In addition to all this take up the shield of faith, with which you can extinguish all the flaming arrows of the evil one.

v. 17, Take the helmet of salvation and the sword of the Spirit, which is the word of God.

v. 18, And pray in the Spirit on all occasions with all kinds of prayers and requests. With this in mind, be alert and always keep on praying for all the saints.'

Six area's Satan uses to destroy the Church:

a) By causing Christians to lie.

Acts 5:3 says,

v. 3, 'Then Peter said, "Ananias, how is it that Satan has so filled your heart that you have lied to the Holy Spirit and have kept for yourself some of the money you received for the land?'

This sin was not one of stinginess or of holding back the money, but rather it was a choice to lie to God and God's people.

Ephesians 4:25 says,

v. 25, 'Therefore each of you must put off falsehood

and speak truthfully to his neighbour, for we are all members of one body.'

Lying to each other disrupts unity by creating conflicts and destroying trust. It tears down relationships and leads to open warfare in the church. If we lie one to another, it causes trouble, friction, disunity and sadness.

b) By tempting Christians in the area of Sexual Sins.

Proverbs 7:6-10 says,

> *v. 6, 'At the window of my house I looked out through the lattice.*
>
> *v. 7, I saw among the simple, I noticed among the young men, a youth who lacked judgment.*
>
> *v. 8, He was going down the street near her corner, walking along in the direction of her house*
>
> *v. 9, At twilight, as the day was fading, as the dark of night set in.*
>
> *v. 10, Then out came a woman to meet him, dressed like a prostitute and with crafty intent.'*

Satan will endeavour to promote the perversion of sex amongst Christians. This is so for both men and women.

In verse 7, it says that this man was simple-minded; he was without aim or direction. He doesn't know where he is heading, but the adulteress knows where she wants him.

1. She dresses to allure (verse 10).
2. Her approach is bold (verse 13).
3. She invites him over (verse 16).
4. She persuades him with smooth talk (verse 21).
5. She traps him (verse 23).

c) By causing Christians to be preoccupied with the sins of the world.

1 John 2:15-17 says,

> *v. 15, 'Do not love the world or anything in the world. If anyone loves the world, the love of the Father is not in him.*
>
> *v. 16, For everything in the world--the cravings of sinful man, the lust of his eyes and the boasting of what he has and does--comes not from the Father but from the world.*
>
> *v. 17, The world and its desires pass away, but the man who does the will of God lives forever.'*

These Scriptures are not referring just to the activities of the world. It refers to an internal desire, a craving of the heart, a 'must have it above anything else' attitude, bowing to materialism. God wants us to be in self-control, to have a spirit of generosity and a commitment to humble service.

1 John 5:19 says,

> v. 19, 'We know that we are children of God, and that the whole world is under the control of the evil one.'

d) By encouraging the sin of reliance on human wisdom and strength.

e) By causing pride in spiritual matters.

When a person is selected for a position or office, he needs to be aware of the damaging effect of pride. Pride can seduce our emotions and cloud our thoughts. If immature, we can come under the influence of unscrupulous people. Remember, pride and conceit were the devils downfall, and he uses pride to trap others.

1 Timothy 3:6 says,

> v. 6, 'He must not be a recent convert, or he may become conceited and fall under the same judgment as the devil.'

It is not good to ordain a novice or recent convert, as the person needs to be proven. Recent converts, may become dangerous. Someone who rises above himself becomes self-confident.

f) By bringing discouragement.

Isaiah 40:31 says,

> *v. 31, 'Yet those who wait for the Lord, will gain new strength; they will mount up with wings like eagles, they will run and not grow weary, they will walk and not faint.'*

If discouragement comes into our lives, we can no longer hear the Word of God, and we no longer worship God. We will have storms in our life. However, we need to be like the eagle. The eagle flies to a high spot to catch the wind, thus enabling it to rise above the storms; whereas the other birds look for a sheltered nest. Look to Jesus as our high spot, and catch the wind of the Holy Spirit, which will take us through (or above) the storms and we'll not become discouraged.

Chapter Seven

THE REALITY OF DEMONS

According to scriptures, the activity of Demons is to: seduce, promote doctrines of uncleanliness, make people sick and promote error.

Whatever view you accept, both views point to their reality. This reality cannot be denied, especially when we begin to look into the Hebrew and Greek names for Demons. Dickason says, 'The names for demons in the Old and New Testament throw light on their existence.'

Let us look at some of these names.

1. Old Testament Names for Demons:

The meaning of the word 'Demon' or 'Devil' or even 'Evil influence', according to Young's Concordance are as follows:

- **Shedhim:** (Deuteronomy 32:17 & Psalm 106:37)

Deuteronomy 32:17 says,

> v. 17, 'They sacrificed to demons, which are not God-- gods they had not known, gods that recently appeared, gods your fathers did not fear.'

Psalm 106:37 says,

> v. 37, 'They even sacrificed their sons and daughters to the demons...'

Dickason writes (in his book Angelology), that the word Shedhim is always in the plural he says this word has the idea of rulers or lords. It speaks of idols as lords, since the Hebrews regarded images as visible symbols of invisible demons. So the Israelites committing idolatry were said to have "sacrificed to demons".

- **Seirim:** (Leviticus 17:7)

The Hebrews were to sacrifice at the altar of the tabernacle and not to sacrifice in the desert to "he goats". Jeroboam the First, appointed worship for the Seirim (2 Chronicles 11: 15) and Josiah broke down the high places of the gates (Shearim) which is to be read Seirim (2 Kings 22:8). These goat-like conceptions (demon-satyrs) were represented as part man and part goat, usually having horns on their heads, a hairy body, with the feet and tail of a goat.

Leviticus 17:7 says,

> v. 7, 'They must no longer offer any of their sacrifices to the goat idols to whom they prostitute themselves. This is to be a lasting ordinance for them and for the generations to come.'

This Scripture shows us that the Israelites were to no longer worship or sacrifice to, the goat idols. The goat idols also called demons were objects of worship and sacrifice in ancient times, particularly in Egypt from which they have escaped. God abhors this type of worship. In 2 Chronicles 11:15 Jeroboam rejected the Levites as Priests and chose his own which were evil priests, being under demonic power.

- **Elilim:** (Psalms 96:5)

This passage identifies demons with idols and suggests demonism. The verse says for all the gods of the nations are idols, only the Lord is worthy of praise.

Psalms 96:4,5 says,

> v. 4, 'For great is the LORD and most worthy of praise; he is to be feared above all gods.

> v. 5, 'For all the gods of the peoples are idols, but the Lord made the heavens.

The only force or power behind an idol is that which a demon gives it. It is not God.

- **Gad:** (Isaiah 65:11)

It is believed the Babylonians worshipped the Demon god 'fortune'. This idolatry was also called the worship of Baal or Bel.

Isaiah 65:11 says,

> v. 11, 'But you who forsake the Lord, who forget my holy mountain, who set a table for Fortune and who fill cups with mixed wine for Destiny.'

Those that forsake the Lord set a table for Fortune.

- **Qeter:** (Psalms 91:6)

Refers to destruction, that wastes at noonday - This was regarded as an evil spirit.

Psalm 91:6 says,

> v. 6, 'Of the pestilence that stalks in darkness, of the destruction that lays waste at noon.'

2. New Testament Names for Demons:

- **Daimon:** This is the word from which the English word demon is derived. Many times demons are mentioned in the New Testament.

For Example:
1. Two possessed men (Matthew 8:28, 31 and Mark 5:12)

2. Spirits of demons who come out of the unholy trinity.
   a) Anti Christ
   b) False prophet (Revelation 16:14)
   c) The Beast

- **Daimonion:** It seems to be a lesser version of Daimon. This was an appropriate term to designate idols and pagan gods.

- **Pheumata:** (Revelation 16:14)

Is apparently intended to distinguish them from human spirits. Not only are they 'unclean spirits' (Verse 13) but they are also not merely human, rather supernatural (spirits of demons): meaning ghostly character of demons. These demons unite the rulers of the world for the battle against God.

Revelation 16:13, 14 says,

> v. 13, 'And I saw coming out of the mouth of the dragon and out of the mouth of the beast and out of the mouth of the false prophet, three unclean spirits like frogs;

> v. 14, For they are spirits of demons, performing signs, which go out to the kings of the whole world, to gather them together for the war of the great day of God, the Almighty.'

- **Angels:** (Matthew 25:41)

The references below of the devil and his angels and also Beelzebub, prince of the devils, seem to equate Satan's angels with demons.

Matthew 25:41 says,

> *v. 41, 'Then He will also say to those on His left, Depart from Me, accursed ones, into the eternal fire which has been prepared for the devil and his angels...'*

Matthew 12:24 says,

> *v. 24, 'But the Pharisees heard it, they said, This man casts out demons only by Beelzebub the ruler of the demons.'*

Note: Beelzebub refers to Satan (Matthew 12:24).

To conclude on the reality of demons, we can see through the scriptures that demons do exist. There is proof of the existence of angels from heathen religions, from the Old Testament and from the New Testament. Basically, the New continues the view of the old regarding demons.

Christ's own views and actions in casting out demons would settle the issue alone. The most common terms in the New Testament for demons are daimonian and Pheumata. The translation "devils" is incorrect, it should be demons - C. Fred Dickason says.

Chapter Eight

The Derivation of Demons

1. The Speculative Theories.

a) Some say that demons are a superstitious way of explaining sickness and disasters in people's lives.

b) Others that demons are departed spirits of ancestors.

c) Others believe that spirits inhabit nature (Confucianism).

d) Evil spirits are called "Jinn" in Islam.

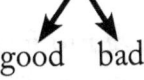
good   bad

e) Also in Islam the word Devils - is Shaiyati and the word Satan - is Shaitin

f) Buddhists also believe in demons.

g) The Persian religion - Zoroastrianism believes in demons.

h) In Aoroastrianism - the demon forces are Angra Maiyu.

i) In Ahura Mazda - They believe in these as good spirits.

2. Supposed Scriptural Theories on The Origin of Demons.

a) Spirits of a Pre-adamic Races.

Demons seek a body to express themselves in. When Satan and his demons were cast out of heaven, the demons came down looking for a body to express themselves in. Finding no physical form, they created a pre adamic race which God destroyed between Genesis 1:1 and 1:2. Now, these ones are seeking to possess human beings again.

b) Spirits of the Monstrous Offspring of Angels and Women.

Genesis 6:1-4 says,

> v. 1, 'When men began to increase in number on the earth and daughters were born to them,

> v. 2, the sons of God saw that the daughters of men were beautiful, and they married any of them they chose.

> v. 3, *Then the LORD said, My Spirit will not contend with man forever, for he is mortal; his days will be a hundred and twenty years.*
>
> v. 4, *The Nephilim were on the earth in those days--and also afterward--when the sons of God went to the daughters of men and had children by them. They were the heroes of old, men of renown.*

This theory believes that demons are the result of the unnatural relationship between women and evil Angels in Genesis chapter 6:1-4. People have thought that the sons of God were fallen angels. These are probably not angels because angels do not marry or reproduce.

Matthew 22:30 says,

> v. 30, *'At the resurrection people will neither marry nor be given in marriage; they will be like the angels in heaven.'*

Some scholars believe this phrase refers to descendants of Seth who intermarried with Cain's evil descendants (the daughters of men) this can weaken the good influence of the faithful, of Seth's line.

These beings were destroyed in the flood, and their spirits seek to possess people today.

3. Substantial Scripture Theory.

Satan and one third of the Angels rebelled against God and were cast out of heaven. They now seek to attack and destroy the lives of men and women: Text 159-160 (from Dickason's book – Angelology)

We favour the theory that Demons are fallen Angels for the following reasons:

a) Similar Relation to Satan.

Beelzebul is interpreted by the Lord Jesus as Satan.

Matthew12:26 says,

> v. 26, 'Moreover, when Beelzebul is designated as 'ruler of the demons.'

The word that is used is "archonti", which has the basic meaning of 'First'. As the first of the demons, he is their ruler.

b) Similar Essence of Being.

Angels are termed "spirits" (Psalms 104:4, Hebrews 1: 14). Demons are also designated as spirits. These are spiritual beings created by God.

1. As God's messengers (Revelation 14:6-12).
2. Executing God's Judgement (Acts 12:1-23 & Revelation 20:1-3).

c) Similar Activities.

Just as Demons seek to enter and control men (Matthew 17:14-18 and Luke 11:14-15), so also may Angels, such as Satan (Luke 22:3, John 13:27). The Demons goal is to control the humans they inhabited. Jesus' goal was to give people freedom from sin and Satan's control.

Mark 5:10 says,

> v. 10, 'And he begged Jesus again and again not to send them out of the area.'

d) Sufficient Identification.

Every mention of Satan's Angels and demons seems to be parallel, and there is no sufficient reason for distinguishing the two.

4. Time of Satan's Fall is supported by three Theory's.

a) Gap Theory of Creation.

Satan fell between Genesis 1:1 & 1:2

b) The Second Theory.

This believes the rebellion of Satan and his Angels took place between Genesis chapter 2 and Genesis chapter 3. Somewhere between where God said the world was good and the temptation of Eve.

c) The Jewish Theory.

The Jews believe that the fall of the one third of the Angels was due to their jealousy and envy of the creation of man.

KNOWING YOUR ENEMY

Chapter Nine

The Description of Demons

☙ ❧

1. Personality of Demons.

Demons are represented in Scripture as intelligent beings.

Mark 5: 10 says,

> v. 10, 'And he begged Jesus again and again not to send them out of the area.'

Luke 4:34 says,

> v. 34, 'Ha! What do you want with us, Jesus of Nazareth? Have you come to destroy us? I know who you are--the Holy One of God!'

Genesis 3:1 says,

> v. 1, 'Now the serpent was more crafty than any of the wild animals the LORD God had made. He

> said to the woman, "Did God really say, 'You must not eat from any tree in the garden'?'

2 Corinthians 11:14 says,

> v. 14, 'And no wonder, for Satan himself masquerades as an angel of light.'

Luke 8:26-36 says,

> v. 26, 'They sailed to the region of the Gerasenes, which is across the lake from Galilee.

> v. 27, When Jesus stepped ashore, he was met by a demon-possessed man from the town. For a long time this man had not worn clothes or lived in a house, but had lived in the tombs.

> v. 28, When he saw Jesus, he cried out and fell at his feet, shouting at the top of his voice, "What do you want with me, Jesus, Son of the Most High God? I beg you, don't torture me!"

> v. 29, For Jesus had commanded the evil spirit to come out of the man. Many times it had seized him, and though he was chained hand and foot and kept under guard, he had broken his chains and had been driven by the demon into solitary places.

THE DESCRIPTION OF DEMONS

v. 30, Jesus asked him, "What is your name?" "Legion," he replied, because many demons had gone into him.

v. 31, And they begged him repeatedly not to order them to go into the Abyss.

v. 32, A large herd of pigs was feeding there on the hillside. The demons begged Jesus to let them go into them, and he gave them permission.

v. 33, When the demons came out of the man, they went into the pigs, and the herd rushed down the steep bank into the lake and was drowned.

v. 34, When those tending the pigs saw what had happened, they ran off and reported this in the town and countryside,

v. 35, and the people went out to see what had happened. When they came to Jesus, they found the man from whom the demons had gone out, sitting at Jesus' feet, dressed and in his right mind; and they were afraid.

v. 36, Those who had seen it told the people how the demon-possessed man had been cured.'

We have the personal pronoun "I" in verse 28, which shows personal identity.

From verses 26-30, we see that the demon has emotions as the Demonic spirits were afraid of Jesus.

In Verses 31-32, they express a desire that they don't want to go into the deep.

Demons have speech, as in verse 28.

2. The Properties of Demons.

Like good angels they exist forever. They are morally unclean (Mark 1:27). In Text 163 they are termed "unclean spirits" Mark 10:1, Mark 1:23, Luke 11:24 or "evil spirits" as in Luke 7:2 I. They are also termed "spiritual forces of wickedness" in Ephesians 6:12. Some are more wicked in their person than others, as shown in Matthew 12:45.

The terminology "unclean" and "evil" is immoral. Demon's immorality is often manifested in the sin of those they control or influence. This may explain the desire of the possessed to live in a state of nudity, to have licentious thoughts (Luke 8:47) and to frequent such impure places as tombs.

They describe themselves as Angels of light and promoters of false doctrine.

Chapter Ten

THE DUTIES OF DEMONS

༄ ༅

1. Promotion of Satan's Program *(Text page 169 - Dickason).*

In general, demons are Satan's untiring and devoted hench-men, organised to accomplish their common purposes.

Satan, by pulling together the resource of many millions of demons, is able to give the appearance that he has all the attributes of God.

2. Opposition to God's Program.

In opposition to God and His program, Satan and his demons use several methods.

First is to promote rebellion in the lives of men and women against God. Moses knew that the Israelites, in spite of all they had seen of God's work, were rebellious at heart. They deserved God's punishment, but received mercy instead. This is the same for us.

Deuteronomy 31:27 says,

> *v. 27, 'For I know how rebellious and stiff-necked you are. If you have been rebellious against the LORD while I am still alive and with you, how much more will you rebel after I die!'*

Second, is to promote slander amongst men, blaming God for circumstances.

Exodus 23:1 says,

> *v. 1, 'Do not spread false reports. Do not help a wicked man by being a malicious witness.'*

Proverbs 25:18 says,

> *v. 18, 'Like a club or a sword or a sharp arrow is the man who gives false testimony against his neighbour.'*

Making up or spreading false reports was strictly forbidden by God! Slander and false witnessing undermine families, churches and friends. We need not circulate rumours.

Third, is to promote ideology.

Fourth, is to hinder men and women from understanding the grace of God.

2 Corinthians 4:4 says,

> v. 4, '... in whose case the god of this world has blinded the minds of the unbelieving, that they might not see the light of the gospel of the glory of Christ, who is the image of God.'

Satan blinds the minds of the people so they won't receive the gospel. Jesus is the Gospel. When we recognise Jesus as Lord, the scales fall off.

An example of this is in John 9:32-38,

> v. 32, 'Nobody has ever heard of opening the eyes of a man born blind.

> v. 33, If this man were not from God, he could do nothing."

> v. 34, To this they replied, "You were steeped in sin at birth; how dare you lecture us!" And they threw him out.

> v. 35, Jesus heard that they had thrown him out, and when he found him, he said. "Do you believe in the Son of Man?"

> v. 36, "Who is he, sir?" the man asked. "Tell me so that I may believe in Him."

> v. 37, Jesus said, "You have now seen him; in fact, he is the one speaking with you."

> v. 38, Then the man said, "Lord, I believe," and he worshipped Him.'

Fifth, is to promote false religion and cults.

2 Corinthians 11: 13-15 says,

> v. 13, 'For such men are false apostles, deceitful workmen, masquerading as apostles of Christ.
>
> v. 14, And no wonder, for Satan himself masquerades as an angel of light.
>
> v. 15, It is not surprising, then, if his servants masquerade as servants of righteousness. Their end will be what their actions deserve.

Satan and his servants can deceive people by appearing to be attractive, good and moral. Many unsuspecting people follow smooth talking, Bible quoting leaders into cults; they lead them from their families and lead them into the practice of immorality and deceit. An example of this is the case of Jim Jones. We need not be fooled by external appearances, and we need to see if the teaching confirms Scripture (Acts 17:11).

> 'v. 11, Now the Bereans were of more noble character than the Thessalonians, for they received the message with great eagerness and examined the scriptures every day to see if what Paul said was true.'

3. Oppression of Mankind.

Demons are employed by Satan for the destruction of mankind. It almost seems that their methods are unlimited.

a) Natural phenomena's.

b) Immorality.

Romans 1: 1 8-32 says,

> v. 18, 'The wrath of God is being revealed from heaven against all the godlessness and wickedness of men who suppress the truth by their wickedness,
>
> v. 19, since what may be known about God is plain to them, because God has made it plain to them.
>
> v. 20, For since the creation of the world God's invisible qualities--His eternal power and divine nature--have been clearly seen, being understood from what has been made, so that men are without excuse.
>
> v. 21, For although they knew God, they neither glorified him as God nor gave thanks to Him, but their thinking became futile and their foolish hearts were darkened.
>
> v. 22, Although they claimed to be wise, they became fools

v. 23, and exchanged the glory of the immortal God for images made to look like mortal man and birds and animals and reptiles.

v. 24, Therefore God gave them over in the sinful desires of their hearts to sexual impurity for the degrading of their bodies with one another.

v. 25, They exchanged the truth of God for a lie, and worshiped and served created things rather than the Creator--who is forever praised. Amen.'

v. 26 Because of this, God gave them over to shameful lusts. Even their women exchanged natural relations for unnatural ones.

v. 27, In the same way the men also abandoned natural relations with women and were inflamed with lust for one another. Men committed indecent acts with other men, and received in themselves the due penalty for their perversion.

v. 28, Furthermore, since they did not think it worthwhile to retain the knowledge of God, He gave them over to a depraved mind, to do what ought not to be done.

v. 29, They have become filled with every kind of wickedness, evil, greed and depravity. They are full of envy, murder, strife, deceit and malice. They are gossips,

v. 30, slanderers, God-haters, insolent, arrogant and boastful; they invent ways of doing evil; they disobey their parents;

v. 31, they are senseless, faithless, heartless, ruthless.

v. 32, Although they know God's righteous decree that those who do such things deserve death, they not only continue to do these very things but also approve of those who practice them.'

4. Physical Ailment.

Demon possession was very active while Jess's was on the earth. Demon possession can cause both mental and physical problems.

In these cases the demons caused:
- Muteness
- Disability of blindness
- Mental Instability

Matthew 9:32-33 says,

v. 32, 'While they were going out, a man who was demon-possessed and could not talk was brought to Jesus.

> v. 33, And when the demon was driven out, the man who had been mute spoke. The crowd was amazed and said, "Nothing like this has ever been seen in Israel."

Matthew 12:22 says,

> v. 22, 'Then they brought him a demon-possessed man who was blind and mute, and Jesus healed him, so that he could both talk and see.'

Luke 13:11-12 says, (demons will cause afflictions and infirmities).

> v. 11, 'And a woman was there who had been crippled by a spirit for eighteen years. She was bent over and could not straighten up at all.

> v. 12 When Jesus saw her, he called her forward and said to her, "Woman, you are set free from your infirmity."

Demons, as we can see, have great destructive power, but when confronted by the name of Jesus, they lose their power. They know who Jesus is. They recognise Him as the Son of God.

Matthew 8:29 says,

> v. 29, "What do you want with us, Son of God?" they shouted. "Have you come here to torture us before the appointed time?"

5. Opposition of the Spirits.

The only way we can withstand the craftiness of Satan is by putting on the whole amour of God. (The concept of the armour is the very armour of God so as to be prepared for battle).

Ephesians 6:10-12 says,

> v. 10, 'Finally, be strong in the Lord and in his mighty power.

> v. 11, Put on the full armour of God so that you can take your stand against the devil's schemes.

> v. 12, For our struggle is not against flesh and blood, but against the rulers, against the authorities, against the powers of this dark world and against the spiritual forces of evil in the heavenly realms.'

6. Over Ruled by God *(Text page 181 - Dickason).*

In all of these activities, God's sovereignty and grace overrules, using them to discipline the believer, defeating the ungodly, and displaying God's righteousness.

KNOWING YOUR ENEMY

Chapter Eleven

DOMINATION OF DEMONS

Demon Possession of Non - Believers and Believers (Text page 182).

The reality of demon possession is clearly stated and described in the New Testament. The apostles and evangelists substantiated the truth of the Gospel by miracles, which included casting out demons (Acts 5:16, 8: 7, 16:16-18,19:12). The enlightened Christian should doubt neither the historicity nor the present possibility of demon possession.

In spite of strong scriptural evidence to support demon possession, a large group of Christians cling to one of the three theories.

1st Theory - The Accommodation Theory.

This theory states that Jesus handled the common people's ignorance and superstitions of demons.

2nd Theory - Mythical Theory.

According to this theory, the casting out of demons was merely symbolic, showing good triumphing over evil.

3rd Theory – Hallucination Theory.

This theory states that the people Jesus healed were not possessed but really worked themselves up into a highly emotional frenzy, and Jesus simply calmed them down.

The Character of Demon Possession

What is demon possession? People who are demon possessed are incapable at times to separate their own conscience and mental process from the influence of a demon.

The word demonised (daimonizomenos), means demon possession.

Matthew 15:22 says,

> v. 22, 'A Canaanite woman from that vicinity came to him, crying out, "Lord, Son of David, have mercy on me! My daughter is suffering terribly from demon-possession.'

Matthew 12:43-45 says,

> v. 43, "When an evil spirit comes out of a man, it goes through arid places seeking rest and does not find it.
>
> v. 44, Then it says, 'I will return to the house I left.' When it arrives, it finds the house unoccupied, swept clean and put in order.

> *v. 45, Then it goes and takes with it seven other spirits more wicked than itself and they go in and live there. And the final condition of that man is worse than the first. That is how it will be with this wicked generation."*

Just cleaning up one's life without filling it with God, leaves plenty of room for Satan to enter. The book of Ezra records how the people rid themselves of idolatry, but failed to replace it with love for God and obedience to Him. Ridding ourselves of sin is the first step. We must take the second step, filling our lives with God's word and the Holy Spirit; unfilled and complacent people are easy targets for Satan.

A person can be demonised by more than one demon. Demon possession brings about a change in a personality. A demon only finds rest when he finds a body.'

A demon that has taken possession of someone's life, will only manifest in a given situation of anger or fear.

Deliverance sometimes comes only by sitting under the Word of God (renewing the mind) or at other times by casting out the demon.

Romans 12:1-2 says,

> *v. 1, 'I urge you therefore brethren, by the mercies of God, to present your bodies as a living and holy sacrifice, acceptable to God, which is your spiritual service of worship.*

> v. 2, 'And do not be conformed to this world, but be transformed by the renewing of your mind, that you may prove what the will of God is, that which is good and acceptable and perfect.'

Mark 16: 15 - 18 says,

> v. 15, 'And He said to them, Go into all the world and preach the gospel to all creation.
>
> v. 16, He who has believed and had been baptized shall be saved, but he who has disbelieved shall be condemned.
>
> v. 17, And these signs will accompany those who have believed: in my name they will cast out demons, they will speak with new tongues;
>
> v. 18, they will pick up serpents, and if they drink any deadly poison, it shall not hurt them; they will lay hands on the sick and they will recover.'

Lists of Actions of Demon Possession

1. Open Doors.

Here is a list of such voluntary actions that not only cause demon possession of ourselves, but can cause demon possession of our loved ones up to the third and fourth generation.

a) Fleshly activities: dope, alcohol, cigarettes and others as listed in Galatians 5:19-21.

> v. 19, 'The acts of the sinful nature are obvious: sexual immorality, impurity and debauchery;

> v. 20, idolatry and witchcraft, hatred, discord, jealousy, fits of rage, selfish ambition, dissensions, factions

> v. 21, and envy; drunkenness, orgies, and the like. I warn you. as I did before, that those who live like this will not inherit the kingdom of God.'

b) Rebellious Attitudes - on a continual basis.

Deuteronomy 21:18 says,

> v. 18, 'If a man has a stubborn and rebellious son who does not obey his father and mother and will not listen to them when they discipline him...'

Jeremiah 4:17 says,

> v. 17, 'They surround her like men guarding a field, because she has rebelled against me," declares the LORD.'

Jeremiah 5:23 says,

> v. 23, 'But these people have stubborn and rebellious hearts; they have turned aside and gone away.'

c) Abnormal Sexual Activity – Homosexuality, etc.

The example of Sodom and Gomorrah is given as a warning for people of all ages. God holds homosexuals fully accountable for their sin.

2 Peter 2:4-10 says,

> v. 4, 'For if God did not spare angels when they sinned, but sent them to hell, putting them into gloomy dungeons to be held for judgment;
>
> v. 5, if He did not spare the ancient world when He brought the flood on its ungodly people, but protected Noah, a preacher of righteousness, and seven others;
>
> v. 6, if He condemned the cities of Sodom and Gomorrah by burning them to ashes, and made them an example of what is going to happen to the ungodly.
>
> v. 7, and if He rescued Lot, a righteous man, who was distressed by the filthy lives of lawless men

> v. 8, (for that righteous man, living among them day after day, was tormented in his righteous soul by the lawless deeds he saw and heard)--
>
> v. 9, if this is so, then the Lord knows how to rescue godly men from trials and to hold the unrighteous for the day of judgment, while continuing their punishment.'
>
> v. 10, This is especially true of those who follow the corrupt desire of the sinful nature and despise authority. Bold and arrogant these men are not afraid to slander celestial beings...'

God condemns homosexuality. Eg. Sodom and Gomorrah.

Genesis 18:20-21 says,

> v. 20, 'Then the LORD said, "The outcry against Sodom and Gomorrah is so great and their sin so grievous
>
> v. 21, that I will go down and see if what they have done is as bad as the outcry that has reached Me. If not, I will know."

d) Through the Family Line - if for example, a parent has been in the occult, etc.

Exodus 20:5 says,

> v. 5, 'You shall not worship them or serve them; for I the Lord your God, am a jealous God, visiting the iniquity of the fathers on the children, on the third and the fourth generations of those who hate Me.'

e) Criticism - (Psalms 102:5, 1 Timothy 2:16-17) - continual and so much a part of your lifestyle.

f) Worry.

Proverbs 12:25 says,

> v. 25, 'An anxious heart weighs a man down, but a kind word cheers him up.'

Proverbs 14:30 says,

> v. 30, 'A heart at peace gives life to the body, but envy rots the bones.'

Proverbs 17:22 says,

> v. 22, 'A cheerful heart is good medicine, but a crushed spirit dries up the bones.'

Worry weighs a person down. Prayer lifts up.

Philippians 4:6-7 says,

> v. 6, 'Do not be anxious about anything, but in

everything, by prayer and petition, with thanksgiving, present your requests to God.

v. 7, And the peace of God, which transcends all understanding, will guard your hearts and your minds in Christ Jesus.'

g) Laziness - the way of a sluggard is hard, more talk and leads to poverty.

Proverbs 15:19 says,

v. 19, 'The way of the sluggard is as a hedge of thorns, but the pathway of the righteous is a highway.'

Proverbs 14:23 says,

v. 23, 'All hard work brings a profit, but mere talk leads only to poverty.'

h) Cults.

Deuteronomy 18:10-11 says,

v. 10, 'Let no one be found among you who sacrifices his son or daughter in the fire, who practices divination or sorcery, interprets omens, engages in witchcraft,

v. 11, or casts spells, or who is a medium or spiritist or who consults the dead.'

i) Rejection and Self Pity.

j) Abnormal Grief.

Proverbs 17:22 says,

> v. 22, 'A cheerful heart is good medicine, but a crushed spirit dries up the bones.'

Psalms 30:5 says,

> v. 5, 'For his anger lasts only a moment, but his favour lasts a lifetime; weeping may remain for a night, but rejoicing comes in the morning.'

k) Fear.

1 John 4:18 says,

> v. 18, 'There is no fear in love. But perfect love drives out fear, because fear has to do with punishment. The one who fears is not made perfect in love.'

l) Hate.

Matthew 5:39,44 says,

> v. 39, 'But I tell you, Do not resist an evil person. If someone strikes you on the right cheek, turn to him the other also.'

> *v. 44, But I tell you: Love your enemies and pray for those who persecute you...'*

A person can become so possessed by demonic forces that it is difficult to determine when they are acting under their own action or the demonic forces. Many times when a person is under demonic forces, their conscience is blocked out and they do not remember what they were doing at that time. One thing is for sure, it is the individual's responsibility to seek help at the time they are conscious of their action. It is then that they have a moral responsibility to themselves and others to do so.

2. Characteristics of Demon Possession:

Koch (Page 185) analyses the story of the Gadarene (Gerasene) demoniac in the book of Mark 5:1-13. He suggests eight distinct symptoms of possession.

a) The indwelling of an unclean spirit (v. 2). This is the cause of the symptoms. It means he was possessed.

b) Unusual physical strength (v. 3).

c) Paroxysms or fits of rage (v. 4) He broke chains and fetters.

d) Disintegration or splitting of personality (v. 6-7) The demoniac ran to Jesus for help, yet cried out in fear.

e) Resistance to spiritual things (v. 7) He asked Jesus to leave him alone.

f) Hyperaesthesia or excessive sensibility such as clairvoyant powers (v7) He knew immediately, without former contact, the true identity of Jesus.

g) Alteration of voice (v. 9) A legion of demons spoke through his vocal facilities.

h) Occult transference (v. 13) The demons left the man and entered into the swine.

Unger also lists several: projection of a new personality, supernatural knowledge (including the ability to speak in unlearned languages), supernatural physical strength, moral depravity. In addition, there may be deep melancholy or seeming idiocy, ecstatic or extremely malevolent ferocious behaviour, spells of unconsciousness, and foaming at the mouth. (Note some of these in Luke 9:39, 42)

From his counselling, Koch lists these: resistance to prayer or Bible reading, falling into a trance during prayer, reaction to the name of Jesus, the exhibition of clairvoyant abilities, and speaking in unlearned languages. He warns those who put so much stress on speaking in tongues that Satan has his counterfeits.

Lechler lists the following: passion for lying and impure thoughts, restlessness and depression and fear, compulsion to rebel against God or blaspheme, violence and cursing, excessive sexual or sensual craving. Resistance and hatred of spiritual things, inability to pronounce or write the name of Jesus, the appearance of mediumistic or clairvoyant abilities, inability to act on Christian counsel, resistance to a Christian counsellor, inability to renounce the works of the devil, seizures or spells of unconsciousness, speaking in unlearned languages, extraordinary physical strength, molestation with pain unrelated to illnesses or injuries. He advises that some of these marks may stem from mere subjection or affliction rather than actual possession, since their marks have much in common.

From the above symptoms listed by counsellors of present day demon-possessed persons, we can see the similarities to biblical examples.

Speaking in unlearned languages is not to be confused with the manifestation of the baptism of the Holy Spirit and its subsequent gifts.

Erickson says - Incidents of demons possession are given prominent attention in the biblical accounts. The technical expression is to "have a demon" or to "be demonised". Sometimes we find expressions like "unclean spirits" (Acts 8:7) or "evil spirits" (Acts 19:12)

People are still possessed by demonic powers today; however this power is broken the same way as it was at the time of the apostles, that is through Jesus Christ.

3. Consideration of Demon Possession of a Christian.

Can a demon possess a Christian?

a) Personal indwelling of the Holy Spirit in regards to demon possession.

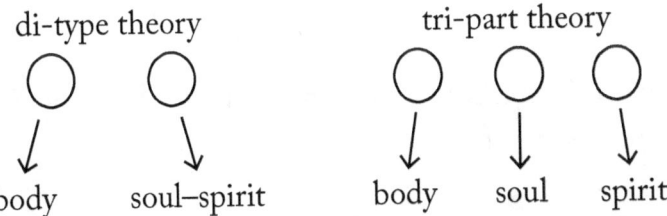

Those who believe that a Christian cannot be demon possessed, base it on their conviction and understanding of Scripture that the soul and spirit are the same (di-type) therefore the demonic power and the Holy Spirit cannot occupy the same place.

Under this: Tri-Part theory – Those who believe that a Christian can be demon possessed believe that the possession takes place in the soulish area. The spiritual area is occupied by the presence of God.

b) Considering Three Words Concerning Demon Possession.

1st - Vexed or Grieved (means that the demon is actually in the person.) It's not total possession but possession of an area of a person.

2nd - Oppressed - refers to being pressed down by force to crush, trample down, overpower, weigh a person down. This is what Satan wants to do to people, weigh them down and overpower them and make them (us) ineffective.

3rd - Possessed - believed to be the same as Vexed. Refers to them being mainly or totally possessed in most areas of a person's life.

4. Powers of Demons

Demonic powers have supernatural strength.

Acts 19:14-16 says,

> *v. 14, 'Seven sons of Sceva, a Jewish chief priest, were doing this.*

> *v. 15, One day the evil spirit answered them, "Jesus I know, and I know about Paul, but who are you?"*

> *v. 16, Then the man who had the evil spirit jumped*

on them and overpowered them all. He gave them such a beating that they ran out of the house naked and bleeding.'

Mark 5:1-4 says,

v. 1, 'They went across the lake to the region of the Gerasenes.

v. 2, When Jesus got out of the boat, a man with an evil spirit came from the tombs to meet him.

v. 3, This man lived In the tombs, and no one could bind him any more, not even with a chain.

v. 4, For he had often been chained hand and foot, but he tore the chains apart and broke the irons on his feet. No one was strong enough to subdue him.'

The demonic powers will counterfeit miracles to deceive people.

KNOWING YOUR ENEMY

CHAPTER TWELVE

THE OCCULT

৸ ৎ

1. The Definition of the Occult *(Text page 196 - Dickason)*

The term occult derives from the Latin "occults", a form of the verb occulere, to cover up, hide. It means hidden, secret, dark, mysterious, concealed.

The occult is divided into three main sections.

a) Divination
It is an attempt to attain secret knowledge, especially of the future either by inspiration or reading and interpreting certain signs called omens.

b) Majic (Magic)
Originally the word meant the science and art of maji. The maji used supernatural power in order to find out the future of mankind.

The word Pharmacy came from an old English word meaning magic portion and witch brew.

The word denotes a society that tolerates hallucinating drugs for satanic observations.

c) Spiritism

It is consulting the spirits of the dead by the use of a medium. The Bible refers to the medium as a Necromancer - Spiritism is a type of witchcraft or black magic.

Deuteronomy 18: 10- 11 says,

> v. 10, 'Let no one be, found among you who sacrifices his son or daughter in the fire, who practices divination or sorcery, interprets omens, engages in witchcraft'

> v. 11, or casts spells, or who is a medium or spiritist or who consults the dead.'

These are not to be a part of the church. When the voice of the dead is heard from a medium it is called "psychic phenomena".

An appearance of a ghost is called "Metaphysical Phenomena". The spirits that mediums contact are spirits, which imitate the dead.

1 Samuel 28:3-19 says,

> v. 3, 'Now Samuel was dead, and all Israel had mourned for him and buried him in his own town of Ramah. Saul had expelled the mediums and spiritists from the land.
>
> v. 4, The Philistines assembled and came and set up camp at Shunem, while Saul gathered all the Israelites and set up camp at Gilboa.
>
> v. 5, When Saul saw the Philistine army, he was afraid, terror filled his heart.
>
> v. 6, He inquired of the LORD, but the LORD did not answer him by dreams or Urim or prophets.
>
> v. 7, Saul then said to his attendants, "Find me a woman who is a medium, so I may go and inquire of her. There is one in Endor." they said.
>
> v. 8, So Saul disguised himself, putting on other clothes, and at night he and two men went to the woman. "Consult a spirit for me." he said, "and bring up for me the one I name."
>
> v. 9, But the woman said to him, "Surely you know what Saul has done. He has cut off the mediums

and spiritists from the land. Why have you set a trap for my life to bring about my death?"

v. 10, Saul swore to her by the LORD, "As surely as the LORD lives, you will not be punished for this."

v. 11, Then the woman asked, "Whom shall I bring up for you?" "Bring up Samuel," he said.

v. 12, When the woman saw Samuel, she cried out at the top of her voice "Why have you deceived me? You are Saul!

v. 13, The king said to her, "Don't be afraid. What do you see?" The woman said. "I see a spirit coming up out of the ground."

v. 14, What does he look like?" he asked. "An old man wearing a robe is coming up," she said. Then Saul knew it was Samuel and he bowed down and prostrated himself with his face to the ground.

v. 15, Samuel said to Saul, "Why have you disturbed me by bringing me up?" "I am in great distress," Saul said. "The Philistines are fighting against me, and God has turned away from me. He no longer answers me, either by prophets or by dreams. So I have called on you to tell me what to do."

v. 16, Samuel said, "Why do you consult me, now that the LORD has turned away from you and become your enemy?"

v. 17, The LORD has done what he predicted through me. The LORD has torn the kingdom out of your hands and given it to one of your neighbours--to David.
v. 18, Because you did not obey the LORD or carry out his fierce wrath against the Amalekites, the LORD has done this to you today.

19 The LORD will hand over both Israel and you to the Philistines, and tomorrow you and your sons will be with die. The LORD will also hand over the army of Israel to the Philistines."

2. The Display of the Occult.

The Occultism has increased in popularity since the age of Aquarius. The popularity of astrology has been caused by the following things:

- Man's personal sense of inadequacy - man's insufficiency, inadequacy, meaning they are not sufficient. There is always a void in a man's life until we come to know Jesus, which brings sufficiency.

- Impersonalisation of society.

- The failure of science to meet man's needs.

- The bankruptcy of religion - need of truth.

- Rebellion against God - is rejection of God (Jesus).

- The opportunity to practice sexual extremes - over doing man's physical need.

3. Denominations of the Occult.

Denominations of the occult are a religious sect or a body, designated by a distinctive name, eg. Jehovah Witness', Mormons, etc.

Occult oppression can be divided into four areas:

a) **Simple subjection** - being under the dominion of another, or a thing or a person exercising lordship.

b) **Domination** - which affects a person unknowingly

c) **Obsession** - continual harassment of Demons - sieging from without, not inwardly - meaning an action of any influence. In this case, a demon or an evil spirit.

d) **Demon possession** - The Demon believes and probably has the right to something that is his. Until Jesus comes and corrects him, he has possession; he has a right to hold onto the person.

The effects of these things:

- Prevents Christians' growth.

- Changes in character can take place.

- Mental and emotional disturbances can occur.

- Tendency towards mental illness.

- Mediumistic ability to contact demons = acting as an agent (mediator), used as an instrument, channel to communicate with departed spirits.

Demon possession can come from three major sources:

a) Inheritance.
God's judgement upon those who get caught up in the occult.

Exodus 20:5 says,

> v. 5, 'You shall not bow down to them or worship them; for I the LORD your God, am a jealous God, punishing the children for the sin of the fathers to the third and forth generation of those who hate me.'

b) Experimentation - drugs.

c) Transference - sexual.

4. Deliverance from the Occult.

Deliverance can take place when the following things happen:

Firstly - The church must recognise that demonic powers do exist. The church must move in the ministry of deliverance. For deliverance to take place, there needs to be fasting, prayer and coming in the Name of Jesus.

You need to be in the right place with God. Prepare yourself for conflict and seek the guidance of the Holy Spirit as to what to do.

Look at Acts 19:13-16,

> *v. 13, 'Some Jews who went around driving out evil spirits tried to invoke the name of the Lord Jesus over those who were demon-possessed. They would say. "In the name of Jesus, whom Paul preaches, I command you to come out."*
>
> *v. 14, Seven sons of Sceva, a Jewish chief priest, were doing this.*
> *v. 15, One day the evil spirit answered them. "Jesus I know and I know about Paul, but who are you?"*
> *v. 16, Then the man who had the evil spirit jumped on them and overpowered them all. He gave them such a beating that they ran out of the house naked and bleeding.'*

Many Ephesians engaged in exorcism and occult practices for profit as seen in Acts 19:18-19.

> *v. 18, 'Many of those who believed now came and openly confessed their evil deeds.*
>
> *v. 19, A number who had practised sorcery brought their scrolls together and burned them publicly. When they calculated the value of the scrolls the total came to fifty thousand drachmas.*

The Sons of Sceva were impressed by Paul's work, whose power to drive out demons came from God's Holy Spirit, not from witchcraft, and was obviously more powerful than theirs. They discovered however, that no one could control or duplicate God's power. These men were calling on the name of Jesus without knowing the person. God works His power only through those He chooses.

Secondly - The person who is demon possessed must take responsibility for recognizing and acknowledging their possession and their need for deliverance.

KNOWING YOUR ENEMY

Chapter Thirteen

THE DEFEAT AND DESTINY OF SATAN AND HIS DEMONS

1. The Defeat of Satan and His Demons:

1 John 3:8 says that Christ came to destroy the works of the devil.

> v. 8, 'He who does what is sinful is of the devil, because the devil has been sinning from the beginning. The reason the Son of God appeared was to destroy the devil's work.'

Three steps are necessary to find victory over prevailing sin:

1. Seek the power of the Holy Spirit and of God's word
2. Stay away from tempting situations
3. Seek help from the body of Christ - prayer

Luke 4:18-19 says,

> v. 18, "The Spirit of the Lord is upon Me, because he has anointed me to preach good news to the poor. He has sent Me to proclaim freedom for the prisoners and recovery of sight for the blind, to release the oppressed,
>
> v. 19, to proclaim the year of the Lord's favour."

Hebrews 2:14 says,

> v. 14, 'Since the children have flesh and blood, He too shared in their humanity so that by His death he might destroy him who holds the power of death, that is, the devil.'

Ephesians 4:8, 9, 10 says,

> v. 8, 'This is why it says: "When He ascended on high, He led captives in His train and gave gifts to men."
>
> v. 9, (What does "he ascended" mean except that he also descended to the lower, earthly regions?
>
> v. 10, He who descended is the very one who ascended higher than all the heavens, in order to fill the whole universe.)'

In Psalm 68:18, God is pictured as a conqueror marching to the gates and taking tribute from the fallen city. Paul uses that picture to teach that Christ in His crucifixion and resurrection was victorious over Satan.

Colossians 1:13 says,

> v. 13, 'For he has rescued us from the dominion of darkness and brought us into the kingdom of the Son he loves.'

True believers have been transferred from darkness to light, from slavery to freedom, from guilt to forgiveness, and from the power of Satan to the Power of God.

Colossians 2:11-15 talks about disarming Satan's authority.

> v. 11, 'In Him you were also circumcised, in the putting off of the sinful nature, not with a circumcision done by the hands of men but with the circumcision done by Christ,
>
> v. 12, having been buried with Him in baptism and raised with Him through your faith in the power of God, who raised Him from the dead.
>
> v. 13, When you were dead in your sins and in the uncircumcision of your sinful nature, God made you alive with Christ. He forgave us all our sins,

> *v. 14, having cancelled the written code, with its regulations, that was against us and that stood opposed to us; he took it away, nailing it to the cross.*
>
> *v. 15, And having disarmed the powers and authorities, he made a public spectacle of them, triumphing over them by the cross.'*

The penalty of sin died with Christ on the Cross. God has declared us not guilty, and we need no longer live under sins power, Satan has no hold on us.

2. The Destiny of Satan and His Demons:

Revelation 20:7-10 says,

> *v. 7, 'When the thousand years are over, Satan will be released from his prison*
>
> *v. 8, and will go out to deceive the nations in the four corners of the earth, Gog and Magog, to gather them for battle. In number they are like the sand on the seashore.*
>
> *v. 9, They marched across the breadth of the earth and surrounded the camp of God's people, the city he loves. But fire came down from heaven and devoured them.*

> *v. 10, And the devil, who deceived them, was thrown into the lake of burning sulphur, where the beast and the false prophet had been thrown. They will be tormented day and night forever and ever.'*

Revelation 19:11-15 says,

> *v. 11, 'I saw heaven standing open and there before me was a white horse, whose rider is called Faithful and True. With Justice He judges and makes war.*
>
> *v. 12, His eyes are like blazing fire, and on His head are many crowns. He has a name written on him that no one knows but He Himself.*
>
> *v. 13, He is dressed in a robe dipped in blood, and his name is the Word of God.*
>
> *v. 14, The armies of heaven were following Him, riding on white horses and dressed in fine linen, white and clean.'*
>
> *v. 15, Out of His mouth comes a sharp sword with which to strike down the nations. "He will rule them with an iron sceptre. "He treads the winepress of the fury of the wrath of God Almighty.'*

Revelation 19:19-21 says,

> v. 19, 'Then I saw the beast and the kings of the earth and their armies gathered together to make war against the rider on the horse and His army.
>
> v. 20, But the beast was captured, and with him the false prophet who had performed the miraculous signs on his behalf. With these signs he had deluded those who had received the mark of the beast and worshiped his image. The two of them were thrown alive into the fiery lake of burning sulphur.
>
> v. 21, The rest of them were killed with the sword that came out of the mouth of the rider on the horse, and all the birds gorged themselves on their flesh.'

Chapter Fourteen

The Defence of Believers Against Satan and Demons

There are three major defences that a believer can use against Satan and his demons.

1. Recall - remember the following things:

a) Man is no match by himself against the power of darkness.

b) Need to be aware of Satan's activities.

c) Christ has purchased our victory at Calvary and prays for us continually.

d) Because of Christ's victory, we have been placed in a position of victory through Christ.

e) God uses Satan for His purposes.

2. Resist.

James 4:7 says,

> v. 7, 'Submit yourselves, then, to God. Resist the devil, and he will flee from you.'

Ephesians 6:10-18 says,

> v. 10, 'Finally, be strong in the Lord and in his mighty power.
>
> v. 11, Put on the full armour of God so that you can take your stand against the devil's schemes.
>
> v. 12, For our struggle is not against flesh and blood, but against the rulers, against the authorities, against the powers of this dark world and against the spiritual forces of evil in the heavenly realm.
>
> v. 13, Therefore put on the full armour of God, so that when the day of evil comes, you may be able to stand your ground, and after you have done everything, to stand.
>
> v. 14, Stand firm then with the belt of truth buckled around your waist, with the breastplate of righteousness in place,

v. 15, and with your feet fitted with the readiness that comes from the gospel of peace.

v. 16, In addition to all this, take up the shield of faith, with which you can extinguish all the flaming arrows of the evil one.

v. 17, Take the helmet of salvation and the sword of the Spirit, which is the word of God.

v. 18, And pray in the Spirit on all occasions with all kinds of prayers and requests. With this in mind, be alert and always keep on praying for all the saints.

The word resist means to make a determined effort to stand against.

3. Rely.

a) To Rely on the power of Christ.

b) Rely on the providence of God / that's God's care and love.

c) Rely on the promises of God.

KNOWING YOUR ENEMY

CONCLUSION

ೞ ಍

Throughout this study, we have found that the Devil does exist.

- We looked at his existence.

- We looked at his fall.

- We found that he was not created evil. He only became evil when pride came into his heart, and wanted to overthrow God.

- He also caused the angels to rebel and betray God.

- Satan or Lucifer misused his position, which brought judgement on himself and on one-third of the angels.

- Satan now has a kingdom, which is the kingdom of darkness (sin).

Matthew 12:26 says,

> v. 26, 'If Satan drives out Satan, he is divided against himself. How then can his kingdom stand?'

Matthew 4:8-9 says,

> v. 8, 'Again, the devil took him to a very high mountain and showed him all the kingdoms of the world and their splendour.
>
> v. 9, "All this I will give you," he said, "If you will bow down and worship me."

Revelation 16:10 says,

> v. 10, 'The fifth angel poured out his bowl on the throne of the beast, and his kingdom was plunged into darkness. Men gnawed their tongues in agony.

1. Satan is called the Evil one.

John 17:15 says,

> v. 15, 'My prayer is not that you take them out of the world but that you protect them from the evil one.'

Ephesians 6:16 says,
> v. 16, 'In addition to all this, take up the shield

of faith, with which you can extinguish all the flaming arrows of the evil one.'

Evil: means deliberate, defiance of moral law for personal gain, without regard to the pain or suffering brought to others by it.

2. Satan is called the destroyer.

Revelation 9:11 says,

> v. 11, 'They had as king over them the angel of the Abyss, whose name in Hebrew is Abaddon, and in Greek, Apollyon.'

The context of this passage of which this verse appears in, is the release of demonic powers held in the bottomless pit, to go forth and torment man for five months. Such is the torment, that man seeks death but won't find it.

Satan's hatred for man is so great that his desire is to inflict pain without regard for the person.

Revelation 12:17 shows us that he has had a hatred for mankind since the beginning.

> v. 17, 'And the dragon was enraged with the woman and went off to make war with the rest of her offspring, who keep the commandments of God and hold to the testimony of Jesus.'

a) His activity in the world is that of being a tempter.

Matthew 4:3 says,

> v. 3, 'The tempter came to him and said, "If you are the Son of God, tell these stones to become bread."

b) To cause affliction and oppression.

Paul was afflicted by a messenger of Satan.

2 Corinthians 12:7 says,

> v. 7, 'To keep me from becoming conceited because of these surpassingly great revelations, there was given me a thorn in my flesh, a messenger of Satan, to torment me.'

Paul opposed Satan when he desired to come to Thessalonica.

1 Thessalonians 2:18 says,

> v. 18, 'For we wanted to come to you; certainly, I, Paul, did, again and again, but Satan stopped us.'

But the good news is that he was conquered by Christ at the cross.

John 12:31 says,

> v. 31, 'Now is the time for judgement on this world; now the prince of this world will be driven out.'

John 16:11 says,

> v. 11, '...and in regard to judgement, because the prince of this world now stands condemned.'

Hebrews 2:14 says,

> v. 14, 'Since the children have flesh and blood, he too shared in their humanity so that by his death he might destroy him who holds the power of death—that is, the devil.'

1 John 3:8 says,

> v. 8, 'He who does what is sinful is of the devil, because the devil has been sinning from the beginning. The reason the Son of God appeared was to destroy the devil's work.'

He and his hosts are being conquered by the church as they release the captives of the human race who are under his control.

Mark 16:15, 20 says,

> v. 15, 'He said to them, "Go into all the world and preach the good news to all creation.'

v. 20, 'Then the disciples went out and preached everywhere, and the Lord worked with them and confirmed His Word by the signs that accompanied it.'

Acts 26:18 says,

v. 18 '...to open their eyes and turn them from darkness to light, and from the power of Satan to God, so that they may receive forgiveness of sins and a place among those who are sanctified by faith in me.'

Romans 16:20 says,

v. 20, 'The God of peace will soon crush Satan under your feet. The grace of our Lord Jesus be with you.'

Yet in all these things we are more than conquerors through Him who loved us!

For I am persuaded that neither death nor life, nor angels nor principalities nor powers, nor things present nor things to come, nor height nor depth, nor any other created thing, shall be able to separate us from the love of God which is in Christ Jesus our Lord.

Romans 8:37-39 (KJV)

ABOUT THE AUTHOR

Brian and wife Judith were both born in New South Wales, but now reside in Queensland.

Brian is a trained Minister, Chaplain and teacher, who believes that people are not reformed, but transformed through the love of Christ.

He has a heart to help those in the community who are struggling with addiction and feel that there is something better than the life they lead.

Using his own life as an example, Brian teaches that what God has done for him, He can do for others.

KNOWING YOUR ENEMY

Also by Brian Hicks

No More Shackles, No More Chains.
No More Shackles No More Chains is the extraordinary life story of Brian Hicks, who in his early years, struggled to find his place in family, society and the workplace.

Available on Amazon,
as well as other online bookstores around the world!

www.ingramcontent.com/pod-product-compliance
Lightning Source LLC
Chambersburg PA
CBHW050312010526
44107CB00055B/2211